Corporate Acquisitions and Mergers in Romania

Corporate Acquisitions and Mergers in Romania

Fourth Edition

Zsuzsa Csiki
Iustinian Captariu
Mihai Stan
Cătălin Roman
Cosmin Vasilescu
Claudiu Ciubotaru
Cătălin Graure
Andrei Gongea
Ioana Popescu
Teodora Nicoschi
Dana Sârbu

Kinstellar SPARL

Edwin Warmerdam
Lucian Dumitru
Cristian Botezatu
Alexandra Nechita

Mazars Tax Consulting SRL

This book was originally published as a chapter in Corporate Acquisitions and Mergers.

General Editor: Peter Begg

Wolters Kluwer

Published by:
Kluwer Law International B.V.
PO Box 316
2400 AH Alphen aan den Rijn
The Netherlands
E-mail: lrs-sales@wolterskluwer.com
Website: www.wolterskluwer.com/en/solutions/kluwerlawinternational

Sold and distributed by:
Wolters Kluwer Legal & Regulatory U.S.
920 Links Avenue
Landisville, PA 17538
United States of America
E-mail: customer.service@wolterskluwer.com

ISBN 978-94-035-3038-3

e-Book: ISBN 978-94-035-3048-2
web-PDF: ISBN 978-94-035-3058-1

Contents

Kinstellar SPARL

Kinstellar is a leading independent law firm in Emerging Europe, Turkey and Central Asia, with offices in eleven jurisdictions (Bulgaria, Croatia, the Czech Republic, Hungary, Kazakhstan, Romania, Serbia, Slovakia, Turkey, Ukraine, Uzbekistan) and more than 350 lawyers. Originating from a magic circle law firm – Linklaters, Kinstellar operates as a single fully integrated firm, delivering consistently high-quality services across the region in an integrated and seamless manner.

Our remit extends to all practice areas including Banking, Finance & Capital Markets, Competition and State Aid, Data & Cybersecurity, Dispute Resolution, Employment & Labour Law, Intellectual Property, M&A & Corporate, Restructuring & Insolvency, White-Collar Crime, and we are particularly well suited to servicing complex transactions for local and international companies active in the sectors: Automotive & Industrial, Consumer & Retail, Defence & Security, Energy & Natural Resources, Financial Institutions, Infrastructure & Transportation, Life Sciences & Healthcare, Real Estate and TMT.

Mazars Tax Consulting SRLMazars is a leading international audit, tax and advisory firm aspiring to build the economic foundations of a fair and prosperous world. Operating as a united partnership, Mazars works as one integrated team, leveraging expertise, scale and cultural understanding to deliver exceptional and tailored services in audit and accounting, as well as tax and financial advisory.

Founded in Europe, Mazars is present in over 95 countries and territories, with over 47,000 professionals – 30,000+ in our integrated partnership and 17,000+ via the Mazars North America Alliance – dedicated to helping clients make the most of business opportunities and operate with confidence.

In Romania, Mazars has twenty-eight years of experience in audit, tax, financial advisory, outsourcing, and consulting. Our strength lies in the people we work with – the local team has seven partners and over three hundred professionals.

Authors

The country chapter on Corporate M&A in Romania has been written by the following team of lawyers of Kinstellar SPARL: Zsuzsa Csiki (Partner – M&A and Corporate, Private Equity, Capital Markets and Financial Regulatory), Iustinian Captariu (Partner – Competition & State Aid, Energy & Natural Resources), Cătălin Graure (Managing Associate – Competition), Mihai Stan (Senior Associate – M&A, Corporate), Cosmin Vasilescu (Associate – M&A, Corporate), Ioana Popescu (Associate – M&A, Corporate), Teodora Nicoschi (Junior Associate – M&A, Corporate), Andrei Gongea (Associate – Competition), Dana Sârbu (Associate – Energy & Natural Resources, Public Procurement and Environmental Law), Cătălin Roman (Senior Associate – Employment Law), Claudiu Ciubotaru (Associate – Employment Law).

The tax and accounting sections have been written by Edwin Warmerdam (Partner, Head of Tax Advisory Services), Lucian Dumitru (Partner), Cristian Botezatu (Senior Manager), Alexandra Nechita (Manager) of Mazars Tax Consulting SRL (Tax Advisors).

Disclaimer

This document does not purport to contain a comprehensive summary of all the legal risks and issues in the legal areas it covers. It is to be used for information only and cannot be relied upon as legal advice; no legal or business decision should be based solely on this document.

1 GEOGRAPHICAL LOCATION

[01] Romania is a mid-sized country located in the southeast of Europe. The country is crossed by the parallel of 45° North latitude and by the meridian of 25° East longitude, being located midway between the North Pole and the Equator and midway between Europe's Western and Eastern extremities.

[02] It is bordered by the Black Sea to the southeast, Bulgaria to the south, Serbia to the southwest, Hungary to the west and Ukraine and the Republic of Moldova to the north and east.

[03] It covers about 238 397 sq. km of land, which makes it a medium-sized European country. Romania is the twelfth-largest country in Europe and the sixth-most populous Member State of the European Union. (It has a predominantly temperate-continental climate and an area of 238 397 km^2 (92 046 sq. mi), with a population of 19 m people (2023). Romania is the twelfth-largest country in Europe and the sixth-most populous Member State of the European Union.

[04] Romania is also at the junction of two prospective transportation corridors: the Orient/East-Med Corridor and the Rhine-Danube Corridor, as approved by EU Regulations no. 1315/2013 and no. 2021/1153.

[05] Its strategic location allows access to countries of the Balkans, the Middle East and North Africa, and also to countries of the former Soviet Union (i.e., Russia and Ukraine).

2 POPULATION AND POPULATION GROWTH

[06] The Romanian population currently amounts to 19 053 815, according to 2023 data, but it continues to decrease. Ethnic Romanian origin is 89.33% of the Romanian population. There is a significant ethnic Hungarian minority representing 6.05% of the total population and also a Romani population which represents 3.44% of the total population. According to the methodology, the proportion of Ukrainians is 0.28%, Germans 0.14%, while the total proportion of other ethnic minorities is 0.77%.

[07] In the previous year, information published by the National Institute for Statistics shows that Romania had a negative population growth. According to the latest information available on the website of the National Institute for Statistics, Romania had an increase of 9.1 thousand persons compared to 1 January 2022.[1]

3 LANGUAGE

[08] The official language is Romanian. However, Hungarian is also widely used in the centre and northwest part of the country.

[1] https://insse.ro/cms/sites/default/files/com_presa/com_pdf/poprez_ian2023r.pdf.

[09] English is widely spoken, especially in urban areas. Other languages, such as French, German, Turkish and Italian, are also spoken by a smaller number of inhabitants.

4 NATURAL RESOURCES

[10] Romania has a wide variety of natural resources, such as:

- deposits of minerals: for example, gold, copper, lead, zinc, manganese, iron, salt, coal;
- good wind potential;
- mineral and geothermal waters;
- good agricultural potential;
- oil and gas; and
- photovoltaic potential.

5 CURRENCY

[11] The national currency is the *leul* (pl. *lei*). In 2005, a currency reform was implemented from the old *leu* (ROL) to the new *leu* (RON), pursuant to which the currency decreased 10 000 times, i.e., four zeroes were removed.

[12] The rules of the National Bank of Romania dictate that payments between residents must be carried out in the national currency. In the case of current and capital transactions between non-residents and residents, the regulations dictate that such transactions may be performed both in foreign and national currencies. Payments may also be made in foreign currency, in certain situations, by the following categories of residents:

(1) legal entities, for payments and cash receipts from cross-border trade of goods and services;
(2) any individual or legal entity, for trading operations inside harbours, airports, customs or on external routes of international trains, ships or aeroplanes;
(3) any individual or legal entity, for operations related to the organization or supply of cross-border services;
(4) individuals, for incidental/occasional operations; and
(5) any individual or legal entity, for operations performed abroad.

[13] The annual average exchange rates for 2023, for EUR and USD, were:

- RON4.9465/EUR.
- RON4.5743/USD.

6 EMPLOYMENT COSTS AND AVAILABILITY OF LABOUR

[14] Employment costs comprise two major components: (i) the salary of the employee; and (ii) the taxes related to the salary which are attributable to the employer and employee.

[15] From 1 October 2023, the minimum gross salary for a full-time job in Romania is RON3 300 (approx. EUR660) or about RON19.960/hour (approx. EUR4/hour). For details regarding the taxes related to the salary, please *see* section *Mandatory Social Contributions* below.

[16] Romania has one of the lowest average hourly labour costs in the EU, i.e., EUR9.5, according to Eurostat statistics.[2]

[17] The unemployment rate has slightly come down to 2.85% in September 2023, as per the data provided by the National Employment Agency.[3]

[18] According to the final results of the 2018 census, persons aged 15 or above were illiterate only 1% (of the total population), meaning that 99% of the population of Romania aged 15 or above are literate (can read and write).[4]

7 INFRASTRUCTURE

[19] Two European transportation corridors will pass through Romania: the Orient/East-Med Corridor and the Rhine-Danube Corridor – provided by EU Regulations no. 1315/2013 and no. 2021/1153. Currently, infrastructure represents one of the weaker points of Romania but is being upgraded. Several construction works for highways have started and are progressing at a reasonable pace. Romania inaugurated 13.5 km of motorway in 2023.

[20] The highway between Bucharest, the country's capital, and Constanta has been finalized, and it is now under operation. This facilitates transportation between Bucharest and Constanta Harbour – the largest harbour on the Black Sea and the 18th largest in Europe.

[21] Additional highways are currently being built in order to connect Constanta Harbour with the western border (i.e., with Hungary). Currently, in Romania, there are 1.118 km of highways in operation and approximately 149 km of highways under construction.

[22] With regard to air transportation, there are sixteen operational airports located around the country. This facilitates movement by aeroplane. The biggest airport is Henri Coanda International Airport located in the country's capital, Bucharest.

[2] Eurostat news release dated March 2023, Labour costs in the EU.

[3] Please refer to the data available on the website of the National Employment Agency.

[4] UIS Data Centre. UNESCO. August 2018. Retrieved 21 Sep. 2021.

8 GOVERNMENT AND POLITICAL SYSTEM

8.1 Political Stability

[23] Romania is organized as a democratic republic, whereby the Prime Minister of Romania is the head of government, and the President of Romania exercises the functions of head of state.

[24] Romania has a multiparty system. However, there are some disputes between the governing party/alliance and the opposition parties, which are somehow normal, bearing in mind the rather large number of parties in the Parliament. Nevertheless, Romania is a politically stable country.

[25] Executive power is exercised by the government. Legislative power is vested in both the government and the two chambers of parliament, the Chamber of Deputies and the Senate.

[26] The judicial system is independent of the executive system and the legislative system.

[27] The right to vote is granted to all citizens over 18 years old.

8.2 Integration into the Global Financial System

[28] As of 1 January 2007, Romania became a member of the EU and, therefore, became subject to the EU Common Trade Policy.

[29] Also, Romania is a founding member of the World Trade Organization, an organization that aims to supervise and liberalize international trade.

[30] The Romanian Government maintains its commitment, through the Convergence Programme for 2021–2024, to fulfil the conditions for and to adopt the Euro as its currency (estimated to become an achievable and necessary goal in 2024–2026). However, the Government's efforts are currently focused on minimizing the negative social and economic effects of the COVID-19 pandemic. The adoption of the Euro as Romania's currency will increase the resilience and flexibility of the Romanian economy.

[31] From the perspective of its successful integration into the global financial system, it is important that a large number of foreign banks are operating in Romania, such as Groupe Societe Generale, Banca Transilvania, Raiffeisen Bank, Credit Europe Bank, Intensa Sanpaolo, ING Bank, BNP Paribas, Citibank Europe and others.

8.3 Membership of Trade Alliances

[32] Romania's investment reputation and climate have been positively influenced by its adherence to: (i) the North Atlantic Treaty Organization in 2004; (ii) the

Organisation for Economic Co-operation and Development (OECD) Declaration and Decisions on International Investment and Multinational Enterprises in 2005; (iii) the EU on 1 January 2007; and (iv) the Global Forum on Transparency and Exchange of Information for Tax Purposes (an organization founded by OECD) in 2013.

[33] Also, Romania is a member of: (i) the International Monetary Fund; (ii) the International Bank for Reconstruction and Development; (iii) the European Bank for Reconstruction and Development; (iv) the Bank for International Settlements; and (v) the Black Sea Trade and Development Bank.

8.4 Entrepreneurship Environment

[34] Romania is currently a very favourable environment for entrepreneurs. The incorporation of a company with the commercial registry, tax and labour authorities takes approximately eight business days (time for gathering information and drafting documents is not included). The Romanian Government has taken significant steps to support the entrepreneurial environment and the Ministry for Entrepreneurs has been set up. Additionally, specific legislation has been passed by the Parliament to encourage and provide tax incentives in case of funding for start-ups coming from business angels.

9 LEGAL SYSTEM

[35] The legal system in Romania is based on civil law. Generally, laws are enforced relatively efficiently by public authorities, although court proceedings can take a significant amount of time before reaching a definitive solution.

[36] Target companies can be identified relatively easily, several important privatizations or secondary public offerings in respect of state-owned entities being conducted through the stock market.

10 CURRENT ECONOMIC ASPECTS

10.1 Growth Rate of Economy

[37] Romania had a negative growth rate of 2.2% of gross domestic product (GDP) in 2023. The growth rate is expected to increase in 2024 to approx. 3%.

[38] Annual *average inflation* was 6.61% in 2023. In 2024, the inflation rate is expected to be higher, averaging 7.00%.

[39] The budget deficit increased to 5.72% in 2023. The forecast is that the budget deficit will decrease to 6.4% of GDP in 2024.

10.2 M&A Trends

[40] The Romanian M&A market neared USD7.1 bn in 2023, based on public sources and disclosed deal values, slightly above the previous year with an increase of 6.1% in value.

[41] The main areas for M&A transactions are: real estate, hospitality and construction, consumer products and retail, technology, high-tech manufacturing, and energy.

[42] In 2024, the M&A market is expected to follow the current upward trend as the appetite for transactions remains high.

[43] On the M&A market in Romania, in 2023, there have been reported 2 transactions of over EUR1 bn – the sale of the Italian Enel Group's operations in Romania to the Greek PPC Group, which paid about EUR1.24 bn for an enterprise value of about EUR1.9 bn (which includes the net debt of the acquired companies), respectively the sale of Profi at an enterprise value of about EUR1.3 bn by the London private equity fund MidEuropa to the strategic investor Ahold Delhaiz.

10.3 Key Industries

[44] The key industries in Romania are:

(1) Automotive.
(2) IT&C.
(3) Agriculture.
(4) Green energy.
(5) Oil and gas industry.
(6) Pharmaceutical industry.
(7) Shipyards.
(8) Telecom sector.
(9) Food and beverages.
(10) Tourism.
(11) Aeronautics.

10.4 Foreign Investment

[45] The Romanian legislation provides national treatment for foreign investors. There was a restriction precluding foreign nationals from acquiring land in Romania, but with effect from 1 January 2014, this restriction was lifted for citizens of the EU or belonging to the European Economic Area (EEA). However, they must still comply with the pre-emption right condition (namely, certain categories of people as defined by law have a pre-emptive right prior to the acquisition of extra-muros agricultural land).

[46] There is no limit on foreign participation in commercial enterprises. Foreign investors are entitled to establish fully owned enterprises in Romania and to convert and repatriate 100% of after-tax profits.

10.5 Role of the State in the Economy

[47] Foreign investments are allowed in all sectors of the economy. However, the State still has the majority stake in a few key companies, such as *Hidroelectrica* (the biggest hydropower producer), *CFR Marfa* (a freight rail company, which will also be privatized in the future), National Airport Company – Bucharest (which operates 'Henri Coanda' International Airport in Bucharest and Baneasa Bucharest Airport) and the Maritime Harbour Administration Constanta (which operates the Constanta Harbour).

[48] In recent years – 2013 – two successful initial public offerings of the State-owned nuclear and natural gas producers, namely *Nuclearelectrica* and *Romgaz*, took place. However, the state still owns the majority stake in both companies. Also, in 2023, *Hidroelectrica* successfully concluded the largest initial public offering ever made on the Bucharest Stock Exchange, in an operation that attracted a total of RON9.28 bn (EUR1.87 bn, USD2.04 bn) for 89.7 m shares representing 19.94% of the total number of shares. However, the state still owns the majority stake in the company.

11 CULTURAL ASPECTS

[49] Generally, Romania is open and welcoming to foreign investment. Doing business in Romania is facilitated by the fact that English is widely spoken and that it offers a well-educated workforce at a competitive cost, a strategic location and abundant natural resources.

[50] However, judicial, legislative and regulatory unpredictability continue to affect the investment climate negatively.

[51] Romania's position at the external border of the EU makes it a target for fiscal crime, including, but not limited exclusively to, cigarette smuggling and infringements of intellectual property rights (IPR). When added to the possibility of value added tax (VAT) fraud and emerging fiscal crimes, the country suffers serious losses to its Treasury.

[52] Most of the European and universal human rights treaties for the protection of human rights have been ratified by Romania. Nevertheless, human trafficking, including forced labour, and discrimination against minority groups remain among the problems Romania faces.

[53] As regards corruption, Romania has made significant progress since 2007. However, Romania still needs to continue to focus on the implementation of key

reforms, including improvements in the management and organization of the judicial system. Also, further efforts are needed to improve the consistency of the case law. To this end, a New Civil Code entered into force in October 2011, and the New Civil Procedure Code entered into force in February 2013. Also, the New Criminal Code and the New Criminal Procedure Code came into force in February 2014.

[54] As regards personal security, it is advisable to maintain at least the same level of awareness as in other countries of the EU.

[55] In Romania, arriving with a small gift when invited to a business meeting by a Romanian partner is considered polite. The gift does not have to be expensive. If the guest is a foreigner, the gift may be a traditional object from the visitor's country. These gifts are considered a sign of international cooperation and are usually opened immediately.

[56] Romanians, just like other people in Eastern Europe in general, are very hospitable.

[57] Business relationships are an important part of the Romanian business culture and have to be maintained and developed in order to succeed. Usually, outsiders are treated rather formally until there has been time to get to know them. After that, once a business relationship is established, it is usually a long-term one based on loyalty and trust.

[58] Romanians are family oriented. Certain events such as birthdays, funerals, marriages and the relevant Orthodox celebrations are important for Romanians.

12 THE CORPORATE REGULATORY FRAMEWORK

12.1 Business Vehicles

[59] Foreign companies seeking to establish a presence in Romania have several options. They can either establish a subsidiary, which is a distinct Romanian legal entity, or a 'secondary office' such as a local branch or representative office. Local 'secondary offices' have no distinct legal personality apart from their foreign parent established abroad.

[60] The most common forms of business vehicles used by local and foreign companies are limited liability companies and joint-stock companies. This is due to the limitation of shareholders' liability to the value of the share capital. Listed companies can only take the form of joint-stock companies and are also subject to specific capital markets rules.

[61] Certain business activities can only be carried out by entities organized in a particular legal form (e.g., asset management, investment firms, insurance and banking entities and non-banking financial institutions can only operate as joint-stock companies).

[62] A company is endowed with legal personality and may start acting as a legal entity upon registration with the local commercial registry.

12.1.1 Registration Formalities

[63] A company is established by filing a constitutive act (in some cases, this must be notarized) and other required documents with the commercial registry.

[64] Generally, the founding shareholders can choose any name for the company as long as the phrases indicating the corporate form are included, namely *societate cu răspundere limitată* (abbreviated to S.R.L.) or *societate pe acţiuni* (abbreviated to S.A.). The statutory restrictions provide that the company name must differ from the names of other registered companies and are subject to public interest restrictions.

[65] The costs of incorporation include, among others, the following:

(1) administrative fees, court fees, public notary fees, which depend on the circumstances of each case;
(2) fees and filing fees in relation to tax registration and licensing; and
(3) if documents are executed/signed abroad, additional costs for certification of signatures by a public notary, legalization and super-legalization or apostille and translation fees apply.

[66] Registration takes about three business days from the date of submission of all relevant documents to the commercial registry.

[67] VAT registration is carried out through a separate procedure before the tax authorities.

12.1.2 Reporting Requirements

[68] From an accounting perspective, legal entities registered in Romania (subsidiaries) are required to keep accounting records in specific registers and to prepare financial statements in accordance with Romanian accounting standards. For example, the financial and accounting documents must be prepared in Romanian and amounts stated in RON (except for the accounting records of foreign operations that must be submitted in both Romanian and foreign currency).

[69] In Romania, thc financial year is the same as the calendar year. However, certain companies and branches of foreign entities can opt for a financial year that is different from the calendar year in order to reflect the financial year used by the parent company. With effect from 2014, those (the profit taxpayers) who opted to use a financial year that is different from the calendar year may opt for the same financial year as the tax year.

[70] As regards tax reporting requirements, the law obliges companies to apply the profit tax regime under certain requirements (this regime is mandatory for all taxpayers who obtained revenues over the threshold of EUR500 000 computed at the National Bank of Romania (NBR) exchange rate valid for the last day of the financial year) and the Romanian branches of foreign companies to submit their annual profit tax return up to 25 March of the following year together with certain information statements concerning the income tax withheld during the previous calendar year. At the same time, all Romanian taxpayers, regardless of legal status, must observe and comply with the tax reporting requirements provided by the Romanian Fiscal Code and the Fiscal Procedure Code: the profit tax/micro-companies tax must be calculated, reported and paid quarterly (or annually in the case of the profit taxpayers), VAT must be declared and paid quarterly or monthly, the salary tax and social security contributions must be declared and paid monthly, etc.

12.1.3 Share Capital

[71] The minimum share capital for joint-stock companies is RON90 000 (approximately EUR18 000), and for limited liability companies is RON1 (approx. EUR0.2). However, in practice, the limited liability companies usually choose a share capital of RON200 (approx. EUR40). There are no maximum share capital requirements.

[72] The initial share capital paid up by the shareholders of a joint-stock company cannot be less than 30% of the entire subscribed capital, while the remaining 70% must be paid within twelve months.

[73] The shareholders of the limited liability company must pay 30% of the share capital after the registration and before the company commences operations (without however exceeding three months from incorporation), and the remaining 70% to be contributed in: (i) twelve months in case of cash contribution; and (ii) two years in case of in-kind contributions, in both cases as of incorporation.

12.1.4 Non-cash Consideration

[74] Cash consideration is mandatory when establishing any type of company. Shares can be issued for contributions in kind, which are evaluated by authorized experts. Restricted contributions include contributions of services or labour and contributions of receivables.

12.1.5 Number of Shareholders

[75] At least two shareholders are necessary for setting up a joint-stock company, with no maximum limit, while a limited liability company can be set up even by a sole shareholder but may have no more than fifty shareholders.

12.1.6 Shares

[76] The share capital of a joint-stock company is divided into shares (Romanian: *actiuni*) of equal value. The nominal value of a share in a joint-stock company cannot be less than RON0.1 (approximately EUR0.02). The constitutive act of a joint-stock company may also dictate that certain shares do not bear voting rights. Shares without voting rights bear priority rights to dividends instead.

[77] The share capital of a limited liability company is divided into shares/social parts (Romanian: *parti sociale*) of equal value. The nominal value of a share in a limited liability company cannot be less than RON1 (approximately EUR0.2). No shares with priority dividend rights may be issued by a limited liability company.

12.1.7 Transferability of Shares

[78] The different types of shares issued by a joint-stock company impact the method of transfer thereof. Thus: (i) registered shares issued in dematerialized form are transferred by registration in the shareholders' registry (by means of a statement registered in the shareholders' register of the company signed by the assignor and the assignee or by their representatives); and (ii) registered shares issued in material form are transferred by registration in the shareholders' registry (as in the case of shares issued in dematerialized form) together with the endorsement of the share certificates by the assignor and the assignee or by their representatives.

[79] In the case of a joint-stock company, the transfer of shares to a third party does not require any formal approval of the other shareholders unless otherwise stated in the constitutive act of the company. Also, it is not mandatory for such transfers to be registered with the commercial registry. However, registration with the commercial registry is advisable in order to ensure enforceability against third parties.

[80] The transfer of shares in a limited liability company to persons outside the company may only be carried out with the approval of shareholders representing at least three-quarters of the company's share capital unless otherwise set forth in the articles of association of the company.

[81] The transfer of shares must be registered with the commercial registry and in the shareholders' register of the company.

[82] The transfer of shares is effective between the shareholders from the date of the resolution of the general shareholders' meeting (GSM) approving the transfer and between the seller and the purchaser from the date of the share purchase agreement.

12.1.8 Rights Attaching to Shares

[83] Voting, dividend and distribution rights (under insolvency and tax laws) can be restricted. Agreements under which a shareholder undertakes to exercise voting rights in accordance with the instructions or proposals of the company, or of the persons representing the company, may be considered void by a court of law.

[84] For joint-stock companies, there is a special category of shares that have priority dividend rights but no voting rights (such shares cannot exceed 25% of the company's share capital).

12.1.9 Automatic Rights Attaching to Shares

[85] Shareholders have the right to:

(1) participate in the general meeting of shareholders and vote on aspects of the corporate life of the company (e.g., the business scope of the company, headquarters, working units, share capital, mergers, acquisitions and spin-offs, dissolution, the issue of bonds, amendment of the company's constitutive act);
(2) appoint and dismiss the directors and auditors of the company;
(3) vote on the budget of the company and approve the financial reports;
(4) cash-in dividends.

[86] Shareholders must exercise their rights within the limits of the company's constitutive act, including any shareholders' agreement.

12.1.10 Joint-Stock Companies: Shareholders' General Meetings

[87] The highest governing body of all joint-stock companies is the GSM. The GSM may be an extraordinary general meeting (in Romanian, *adunare generală extraordinară*) or an ordinary general meeting (in Romanian, *adunare generală ordinară*).

[88] Ordinary *GSMs* are to be held at least once a year, upon the elapse of five months, at the latest, from the end of the previous fiscal year or whenever necessary. Their main purposes are to approve the previous fiscal year's financial statements and any profit distribution, to declare dividends to be distributed to the shareholders, to appoint or remove the auditor (as the case may be), to appoint and remove members of the board of directors (in Romanian, *consiliul de administraŢie*) and/or the supervisory council (in Romanian, *consiliul de supraveghere*) as the case may be, to approve the yearly budget, to render decisions relating to the pledging or mortgaging of the company's units and other matters.

[89] Ordinary GSMs may be convened by the board of directors directly or at the request of shareholders representing at least 5% of the company's registered capital. Ordinary GSMs are validly convened if at least 25% of the total voting rights are present at the first calling, or any percentage at the second calling. Ordinary GSM decisions are approved by a simple majority of the voting rights which are actually exercised (i.e., abstentions are not taken into account).

[90] *Extraordinary GSMs* are convened whenever necessary. The main purposes of an extraordinary GSM are to change the company's corporate form, to change the registered seat, to change the company's scope of activities, to increase or decrease the share capital, to approve a spin-off or merger, to approve the voluntary dissolution of the company, to issue bonds, to convert shares from one category to another, to convert one category of bonds to another category or into shares, to modify the company's constitutive act and other matters. Nevertheless, the right to increase the company's share capital, to change the headquarters and to amend the secondary business scope may be delegated to the company's board of directors or to the management board, as the case may be.

[91] *Extraordinary* GSMs may be convened by the board of directors directly or at the request of shareholders representing at least 5% of the company's registered capital. Extraordinary GSMs are validly convened if at least 25% of the total voting rights are present at the first calling or 20% at the second calling. Most decisions are subject to a simple majority (50%+1) of the voting rights; however, those relating to a change of the main scope of activity, an increase or decrease of the share capital, a change of corporate form, or the approval of a merger, spin-off or voluntary dissolution require a two-thirds majority, with the possibility for higher quorum and voting thresholds to be stipulated in the constitutive act.

[92] Law no. 31 of 1990 on companies (the '*Company Law*') requires that shareholders be informed of a shareholders' meeting as indicated in the company's constitutive act. The convening of a GSM must be published in the Official Gazette of Romania as well as in a widely circulated newspaper from the municipality where the company's headquarters is located at least thirty days prior to the date of the GSM. The foregoing convening formalities may be waived by the unanimous consent of shareholders representing 100% of a company's registered capital, which may convene and hold a shareholders' meeting without these formalities. The GSM may take place at the company's headquarters or at any other location in Romania or abroad.

[93] At the GSM, shareholders may be represented either by other shareholders or by third parties who are authorized pursuant to a special proxy. Legal entity shareholders may be represented in the GSM by their legal representatives with signatory authority, who in turn may grant special proxies to other persons. Company directors, managers and other executive personnel are not allowed to represent shareholders. The right to vote may not be assigned, and the company or its management are forbidden to instruct shareholders on how to vote.

12.1.11 Joint-Stock Companies: Management Bodies

[94] Joint-stock companies may implement either a one-tier or a two-tier management system.

[95] Under the one-tier system, the company would be run by a board of directors (in Romanian, *consiliu de administraŢie*), which can choose to (or in certain circumstances must) delegate the management of the company to officers (in Romanian, *directori*), who may also be members of the board of directors. Under the two-tier system, the company would be run by a supervisory council (in Romanian, *consiliu de supraveghere*) and a management board (in Romanian, *directorat*). Under such a system, the supervisory council's tasks involve only non-executive and administrative-type of duties, whereas the management board is solely responsible for executive tasks and the company's day-to-day operations.

[96] Members of management bodies, irrespective of the chosen system, must not be employees of the company during their mandate (meaning, in practice, that

they must not be carrying out their duties pursuant to an employment agreement registered with the relevant labour inspectorate). If a member of a management body would also be an employee at the time of the appointment, his/her employment agreement would be suspended during his/her mandate. Likewise, members of management bodies, irrespective of the chosen system, are required to obtain D&O insurance (i.e., insurance against personal liability for losses incurred by a third party due to the negligent discharge of duties by the company's directors or management team).

[97] The mandate of each director cannot exceed a timeframe of more than four years, and they can be re-elected unless otherwise provided in the constitutive act. The mandate of the first directors cannot exceed two years, with the possibility of re-election.

One-Tier System

[98] Under the one-tier system, the members of the board of directors are appointed and dismissed by the ordinary general meeting of shareholders. There is also the possibility of appointing a sole director, except for companies whose financial statements must be audited, in which case, at least three directors are required. There must always be an odd number of directors. The board of directors has full powers to run the company's operations within the limits of the scope of activity, except for those issues falling under the competence of the GSM according to the applicable law or the company's constitutive act. The board of directors may set up consultative committees (such as audit and compensation committees) formed by at least two board members, one of whom must be an independent member. The board of directors is also required to formally meet at least once every three months.

[99] A company with the obligation to audit its financial statements must delegate management duties to one or more executive officers and appoint one of these officers as the chief executive officer (CEO). However, the following matters fall within the exclusive competence of the board of directors and may not be delegated to the officers: (i) establishment of the principal business and development strategy/plans; (ii) establishment of the company's accounting system and system of financial controls as well as the approval of financial planning matters; (iii) appointment and dismissal of executive officers and establishment of their remuneration; (iv) supervision of the executive officers' activities; (v) drafting of the annual report, convening of a GSM and implementation of the rendered decisions; (vi) commencement of insolvency proceedings; and (vii) those powers delegated to the board of directors pursuant to a GSM.

[100] Executive officers have full management powers within the limits of the scope of activity of the company and in compliance with the limitations set out in the constitutive act. Executive officers may also be appointed as directors, although in cases where one or more directors are also officers (executive directors), the majority of board members must be non-executive directors.

Two-Tier System

[101] Under the two-tier system, the supervisory council is appointed by the shareholders, with this council comprising between three and eleven persons, who may be revoked at any time by the shareholders pursuant to a GSM decision approved by two-thirds of those present and voting. The supervisory council may not be delegated with any activities involving the company's operations. However, the constitutive act may stipulate that certain operations may be performed with the consent or approval of the supervisory council only. In addition, the supervisory council may create consultative committees (such as audit and compensation committees) formed by at least two council members, one of whom must be an independent member. Finally, the supervisory council is also required to formally meet at least once every three months.

[102] The members of the management board are appointed and dismissed by the supervisory council. The management board comprises one or more members (one of which is the general manager), and it has an odd number of members. A company that is required to audit its financial statements must have at least three members. The members of the management board may not be members of the supervisory council.

[103] The management board has full management powers within the limits of the scope of activity of the company and in compliance with the limitations set out in the constitutive act. The management board carries out the management of the company and must submit to the supervisory council every three months a written report on the company's activities and projected forecasts. The management board is obliged to submit to the supervisory council the annual financial statements and annual report and to make proposals regarding the distribution of profits.

[104] The two-tier management system is not commonly used in practice and is usually implemented by large companies, while other joint-stock companies set up a similar form of management by delegating the powers of the board of directors to executive managers (executive officers).

12.1.12 Limited Liability Companies: Shareholders' General Meetings

[105] Limited liability companies are governed by the shareholders through the GSM.

[106] The GSM is the supreme governing body of a limited liability company. As opposed to joint-stock companies, there is only a single type of GSM, with no distinction between ordinary and extraordinary meetings. The GSM has the following powers:

(1) to approve the annual financial statement and establish the distribution of the net profit;

(2) to appoint and revoke the directors and censors (in such cases), to discharge them from liability and to decide the appointment of the financial auditor when such appointment is mandatory pursuant to the law;
(3) to assess the performance of the directors and to file claims against the directors and the censors (in such cases) for damages caused to the company; and
(4) to amend the constitutive act of the company.

[107] The GSM is convened by the directors at least once a year. The directors must also convene the GSM at the request of one or more shareholders representing at least 25% of the share capital.

[108] Unless otherwise provided in the constitutive act, the GSM decides by majority vote (double majority of the number of shares and of the number of shareholders), unless the constitutive act provides otherwise. If the necessary majority is not achieved at the first meeting, a second meeting is allowed to make the decision irrespective of the number of shareholders present. Shareholders cannot vote on matters regarding transactions between themselves and the company or the valuation of their contributions in kind.

[109] A GSM decision which approves changes or amendments to the constitutive act of the company must be registered with the relevant commercial registry, in order to be enforceable against third parties. The relevant commercial registry will further send the GSM decision for publication in the Official Gazette of Romania.

12.1.13 Limited Liability Companies: Directors

[110] The management of a limited liability company is carried out by one or several directors (either individuals or legal entities). As opposed to joint-stock companies, a director in a limited liability company may be appointed for longer periods of time (such as five years, ten years, fifteen years, etc.). Unlimited mandates are not accepted.

[111] As a matter of practice, if the limited liability company has several directors, the constitutive act of the limited liability company may dictate that the management of the company is carried out by a board of directors similar to that of a joint-stock company. Note that where the limited liability company has more than one director, the setting up of a board of directors by the company is not required by the Company Law.

[112] As opposed to joint-stock companies, in respect of which the possibility for the director/board of directors to delegate executive powers to a manager is expressly set out in the Company Law, for limited liability companies, the Company Law generally states that the representation powers may be delegated.

[113] Directors in a limited liability company may delegate executive powers to managers to the extent the constitutive act allows them to do so.

[114] Directors are appointed and dismissed by the general meeting of shareholders. There is no restriction as to the number of directors. Directors have full powers to run the company's operations within the limits of the company's scope of activity, except for those falling within the exclusive competence of the GSM according to the Company Law or the company's constitutive act. Unless otherwise stipulated in the constitutive act, each director has the right to independently sign on behalf of the company (meaning without the joint signature of another director).

[115] It is important to note that from a corporate governance point of view, none of the requirements or restrictions applicable to directors of joint-stock companies is applicable to directors of limited liability companies.

12.1.14 Subsequent Registration of Changes to the Constitutive Documents

[116] Within the context of mergers and acquisitions, transactions involving changes to the constitutive act of a company or changes to the board of directors (or other corporate bodies) will require a shareholders' or members' meeting. The Company Law further dictates that in the event of any changes to the constitutive act, the modified constitutive act must be registered with the competent trade registry. As regards listed companies, all decisions approved pursuant to a general meeting of shareholders must also be reported to the Romanian Financial Supervisory Authority (FSA) and the relevant exchange.

[117] Normally, directors of joint-stock companies or limited liability companies exercise executive authority. As long as the representation powers, as provided by the Company Law or by the company's constitutive act, are observed, there is no supplemental specific document required in this respect. However, a scenario whereby a third party is empowered to exercise executive authority may also be contemplated, provided the relevant conditions are observed as appropriate to each particular situation (e.g., a power of attorney signed before a public notary or under a private deed; powers of subdelegation granted to legal representatives).

12.2 Laws Affecting M&A

[118] M&A activity is generally regulated and influenced by several local laws and regulations, for example: (i) the Company Law (Law 31/1990) – on establishing and operating commercial companies; (ii) the Civil Code (Law 287/2009) – on the Romanian common civil framework; (iii) the Fiscal Code (Law 227/2015) – on the common fiscal framework applicable to Romanian transactions; (iv) the Labour Code (Law 53/2003), Law 367/2022, Law 67/2006 – on employment matters; (v) the Capital Markets Law (Law 297/2004) – on capital markets matters; (vi) the Law on issuers of financial instruments and market operations (Law 24/2017) (point (v) and (vi) being together referred to herein as Capital Markets Laws); or (vii) the Banking Law (Government Emergency Ordinance (GEO) 99/2006) – on bank institutions matters.

12.2.1 Industry-Specific Regulatory Schemes

[119] There are strict rules that apply to certain industries. For instance, pension funds, insurance companies and banks are all subject to strict limitations concerning the principles applicable to their activity, the types of investments they may opt for and the size of the investment itself. This careful regulation is dictated by the fact that, unlike other entities, they have a declared mission to multiply the amounts received from contributors to be able to reimburse the contributors according to a specific scheme (interest, pension, insurance premiums, etc.).

[120] Further regulatory requirements and approval processes apply to participation thresholds and investor targets in investment firms, insurance companies and banks under the laws implementing the Acquisitions Directive.

12.2.2 Regulatory Bodies

[121] An M&A transaction may trigger the involvement of several regulatory bodies, which usually have a significant impact on the timing and procedural steps thereof. Some of the regulatory bodies most commonly involved in M&A transactions include, for example: (i) the Commercial Registry – regulating specific requirements/steps of corporate registrations; (ii) the National Bank of Romania – on the banking sector; (iii) the FSA – an independent regulatory agency overseeing the market and issuing secondary legislation regarding the Capital Markets Laws; (iv) the Bucharest Stock Exchange (BSE) – the only regulated market that currently operates in Romania; or (v) the Competition Council – an independent administrative authority regulating all competition-related issues, especially those regarding merger controls and foreign direct investments.

12.2.3 Private/Public Transactions

[122] Romanian law is very permissive with respect to private equity transactions. All types of private equity transactions may be implemented in Romania, including management buyouts, leveraged buyouts, mergers and acquisitions (sale of shares or assets, or both). However, even if, theoretically, a multiplicity of different possible structures could be contemplated, as a matter of practice, private equity transactions are usually transacted as a sale of shares.

[123] Transactions involving public companies (companies listed on the BSE) are separately regulated by the Romanian FSA, which must approve the offer prospectus before it is made public. This approval does not assess the merits of the purported transaction; it only states whether the offer is consistent with the conditions prescribed by the law (e.g., as to the price). This conservative procedure remains complicated and bureaucratic and inconsistent with the introduction of the dualistic management system, which is therefore left without an important function.

12.2.4 Hostile Bids

[124] Hostile bids are not explicitly regulated by the Company Law, but they are legally permissible under the Capital Markets Laws. The way the target's board of directors reacts to an intended takeover determines whether the bid is a friendly or a hostile one. The board's reaction is likely to be negative if it threatens the well-being of the shareholders or the board's position after the proposed takeover.

[125] Hostile bids are not common, as they rarely endanger the position of the target's board members and usually offer significant benefits to the shareholders, triggering a positive rather than a negative opinion by the board. In addition, given the fact that Romania's corporate culture is still developing, shareholders are relatively unaware of their ability to act together against hostile bidders.

[126] The local market is continuously diversifying in Romania and becoming more and more mature with respect to ways of structuring a transaction. Parties seek to find and apply the most appropriately tailored solution, whether this means a share transaction, an asset deal, a merger or spin-off or a transfer of business. In any event, since 2007, the majority of mergers and acquisitions in Romania have involved share transactions or asset deals and have been private-to-private transactions.

[127] More complex transactions typically encountered in Western Europe and the United States (US), such as leveraged buyouts, hostile bids and proxy fights, remain the exception in Romania.

12.2.5 Share Deals

[128] The number of share deals has exponentially increased in Romania since 2003, and a typical share deal involving a foreign party will be quite similar to one carried out in Western Europe or the US. It has now become standard practice to commence such a transaction with an English language memorandum of understanding or letter of intent, for the target to undergo a tax and legal due diligence procedure, and for the parties to negotiate a share purchase agreement which includes a substantial number of representations and warranties (with tax representations and warranties usually being in effect for five years from the effective date of the agreement, while the other representations and warranties generally remain in effect for three years). Likewise, arbitration clauses are also increasingly being used, given that the Romanian court system remains slow and unpredictable.

[129] From a taxation point of view, unless exempted under a double taxation treaty, the sellers are taxed on their capital gains at a rate of 16%, and in the event that the purchaser is a foreign legal entity and the seller is a Romanian natural person, a fiscal representative will have to be appointed by the purchaser who is responsible for withholding the 16% capital gains tax and for paying the relevant amount to the Romanian tax authorities.

12.2.6 Asset Deals

[130] Asset deals are also quite common nowadays in Romania and similar to share deals in that if a foreign party is involved, then the language of the documentation is frequently English.

[131] Generally speaking, it is possible to structure an asset deal so that it is tax neutral pursuant to the Fiscal Code.

12.2.7 Shareholders' Agreements

[132] Shareholders' agreements have also become a standard document in share deals. Nonetheless, although these types of agreements usually include call and put options as well as tag along and drag along rights, these types of clauses have largely remained untested under Romanian law and the local courts. One of the major problems in this respect is that it is not possible in Romania to issue an irrevocable power of attorney (which is a key instrument in the exercise of such rights). This means that the enforcement of such types of rights would, in any event, require court action if one of the parties were to withdraw a power of attorney or were to refuse to execute the necessary documents for the registration of the transfer of shares in the relevant company's shareholders/members registry and/or the competent trade registry. In any event, it is difficult to assess with any accuracy whether Romanian courts would order specific performance with respect to such rights or would only award damages for the breach of such clauses.

[133] *Mergers*. Romanian law regulates two types of merger processes: merger by absorption, whereby a company absorbs one or more companies that cease to exist, and merger by consolidation, whereby two or more companies which cease to exist establish a new company. Romanian companies are allowed to merge with EU-based companies.

[134] *Spin-offs*. The shareholders of a company may resolve upon: a total spin-off, whereby the total assets and liabilities of a company, which ceases to exist, are split up between two or several already existing companies or start-ups specifically set up for this purpose; or a partial spin-off, whereby only part of the assets and liabilities of a company, which continues to exist, are transferred to two or several already existing companies or start-ups.

[135] *Transfer of business*. Shareholders may also decide to transfer an entire line of business to a designated purchaser. Entering into this type of agreement is usually accompanied by a restriction incumbent on the sellers and the company to engage in identical lines of business. Extra care should be paid to the protection of employees and to the proper scrutiny of the covenants and undertakings from a competition law perspective.

[136] *Cooperation structures deprived of legal capacity*. Investors seeking tailor-made solutions for specific projects often choose to put together certain assets and create a joint venture instead of a project company. The joint venture, created pursuant to a joint venture agreement, is not a stand-alone legal entity, and one of the partners

is appointed as the leading partner of the joint venture, charged with representing all the partners' interests in relation to third parties and with the bookkeeping of the joint venture.

12.3 Relevant Regulatory Authorities

[137] For the main regulatory bodies and a general description of their respective mandates, please refer to the section *Laws affecting M&A*.

[138] Implementing an M&A transaction prior to having obtained the required approvals/permits/licences/endorsements and prior to implementing the relevant registration formalities with the relevant authorities, as the case may be, is restricted.

[139] Deadlines provided by law vary depending on the type of approval/registration and on the authority concerned. For the authorities listed under the section *Laws affecting M&A*, such legal terms may range from three days (for registering a company with the Commercial Registry) to five months (for the authorization of an economic concentration by the Romanian Competition Council (RCC) if an investigation in respect of the operation of concentration has been deemed necessary).

[140] In the absence of a specific deadline provided by law, the legal term for a Romanian authority to respond to a request is thirty days.

[141] Although the degree of compliance with the legal deadlines has greatly improved during the past years, in practice and depending, in particular, on the workload of the relevant authority, the actual process may, in some cases, still take longer than required by the law.

[142] In general, the legal deadline begins to run upon submission of the *complete* file to the satisfaction of the relevant authority.

[143] In this respect, it is noteworthy that Romanian authorities often request additional documents, which are not always indicated in the relevant legal provisions but may be set out in internal norms (not published in the Official Gazette) or may be a matter of practice of the authority concerned.

[144] It is therefore advisable, in order to increase the chances of expediting the approval process, to make all efforts to ensure that the file is as correct and as complete as possible.

[145] For this purpose, a very good option is to have a local partner or advisor with extensive knowledge of the relevant sector and of the relevant authority's practice.

[146] While it remains possible to personally engage with regulatory authorities, many investors (especially those present for the first time in Romania) prefer recourse to local advisors due to their knowledge of regulations and authority practice in the relevant sector. Nonetheless, the opposite approach of personally getting involved in the approval process is sometimes used. If the local acquisition target is a bank or an investment firm, it is advisable and appropriate to contact the regulator in advance of the filing to explain the transaction. To this end, a formal meeting is recommended to be set up with the relevant authority in order to provide the regulator with a 'heads-up' regarding the anticipated transaction steps and to streamline any issues regarding the availability of information and documentation that may be required in relation to the transaction approval process.

12.4 Controls/Restrictions on Foreign Investment

[147] Romania has enacted a new foreign direct investment ('**FDI**') screening regime meant to ensure the application at local level of the EU FDI Regulation 2019/452 (the '**EU FDI Regulation**'), particularly focusing on foreign investments from outside the EU, but as of late, also capturing investments from within the EU, as well as purely local investments. The new FDI regime was enacted through the adoption of Government Emergency Ordinance no. 46/2022 ('**GEO no. 46/2022**'), which entered into force on 18 April 2022.

[148] Under the new FDI regime, the FDI screening is done by a newly formed FDI Screening Commission ('**CEISD**'). In this regard, although the new FDI law entered into force on 18 April 2022, the CEISD was formally set up only on 6 June 2022. The secondary legislation needed for the application of the new FDI regime, which also serves as a regulation for the functioning of the CEISD, was adopted on 8 November 2022.

[149] In brief, for a transaction to trigger an FDI filing obligation in Romania, the following cumulative criteria must be met:

- there must be an investment of any kind by an investor in view of establishing or maintaining lasting and direct links between the investor and the entrepreneur to whom or undertaking to which the capital is made available in order to carry on an economic activity in Romania, including investments which enable effective participation in the management or control of a company carrying out an economic activity;
- we also note that greenfield investments and extending the capacity or diversifying the production of existing undertakings would also generally fall within the scope of the new FDI screening regime;
- the investment must fall under a broadly defined list of sensitive sectors under Decision no. 73/2012 of the Supreme Council for National Defence (i.e., (a) agricultural and environmental protection, (b) arms, ammunition, explosives and toxic substances (production and transportation), (c) border security, (d) critical infrastructure, (f) energy security, (g) financial, tax, banking and insurance activities, (h) hazard protection, (j) industrial security, (k) IT and communications systems, (l) protecting the privatization of State-owned undertakings or their management, (m) the security of citizens and collectivities, (n) transport security and (o) vital resources supply), while the factors under Article 4 of the EU FDI Regulation would also be considered for the national security analysis; and

- the value of the investment must exceed EUR2 m. The law does not provide clear guidance on how the investment value would be calculated, but this is expected to be further clarified in the future under the secondary legislation to the new FDI regime.

[150] Moreover, there is a clear standstill obligation and fines of up to 10% of the investor's annual global turnover in the year preceding the sanctioning decision for gun jumping the FDI filing obligation, and there are also risks of having the transaction unwound (if deemed to have affected national security or public order). In this respect, gun jumping could generally mean implementing/closing a transaction/investment prior to obtaining the FDI clearance.

[151] The new law also provides that a separate FDI filing would need to be made if the filing criteria are met, regardless of whether the respective transaction would also be notified to the RCC for merger control review. Therefore, where a transaction meets both sets of criteria, two separate filings would be needed, i.e., to the CEISD for the FDI clearance and to the RCC for the merger control clearance.

[152] In terms of the process for clearance, for a phase I, no-issues case, the FDI law provides for up to 135 calendar days for the authorities to grant the clearance, which starts running as of the date the filing is deemed complete (i.e., not necessarily from submission). The formal FDI clearance decision is issued by the RCC based on the clearance opinion given by the CEISD. As regards the screening of investments by EU investors, GEO no. 46/2022 was amended in December 2023 through Government Emergency Ordinance no. 108/2023 and provided for a fast-track screening and clearance of up to seventy calendar days for a no-issues case. In such instances, the RCC only issues the investor a clearance letter and no longer has to draft and communicate a clearance decision, which may be expected to streamline the process.

[153] Where the CEISD considers that remedies are necessary for an investment to be approved or in cases where it concludes that the notified investment would raise issues to Romania's national security or public order or would affect projects or programmes of interest to the EU, its opinion on the matter would be forwarded for the Government's analysis (under a Phase II process) and it would be the Government issuing the formal decision in this respect (i.e., clearing the proposed investment subject to remedies (either structural or behavioural) offered by the investor, or prohibiting the investment, as applicable). The law does not provide for a maximum duration for such a Phase II analysis.

[154] Through the same ordinance amending GEO no. 46/2022 in December 2023, an EUR10 000 filing fee was introduced. The so-called screening contribution is payable upon filing and is to be returned to the investor in case the authorities conclude that the notified investment did not fall under the scope of the FDI law.

[155] In terms of restrictions on ownership of land, since 1 January 2014, the relevant restrictions only apply to non-EU individuals and companies. Individuals and companies from the EU are entitled to acquire land on the same terms as

Romanian citizens and companies. For *extra-muros agricultural land, a prior pre-emption right is applicable and prior endorsement is mandatory, but under the same conditions as for Romanian citizens and companies.*

12.5 Incentives for Foreign Investment

[156] Foreign investors in Romania may benefit from several types of incentives and tax facilities, the most significant being the following.

12.5.1 State Aid Incentives: State Aid

[157] In view of the fact that state aid is generally not allowed pursuant to the general principles of the EU's single market, Romania has severely amended its state aid policy after the country's accession to the EU in 2007, with a view to ensuring compliance with the strict state aid rules stipulated in the EU legislation.

[158] Romania has implemented several state aid schemes in compliance with the EU legislation, subject to prior notification of the European Commission, which is the entity authorized to decide upon the implementation or suspension of state aid measures.

[159] State aid is applicable in Romania to small and medium-sized companies, as well as to large companies, depending on the type of investment and the relevant state aid scheme. Pursuant to the domestic procedure applicable to state aid, new state aid may be approved only after the notification of the European Commission by the Romanian Competition Council has been completed, which must first issue conformity advice with respect to the relevant state aid programme.

[160] In order to benefit from state aid incentives, investments should fulfil various specific conditions related to the amount, duration, objectives and eligibility, depending on the relevant scheme.

[161] A noteworthy state aid programme was initiated in Romania in May 2014 for investments promoting regional development and creation of jobs, which was later extended until 2023. Financing under this state aid scheme was granted to companies which directly generated jobs: (i) through investment projects, (ii) after receiving the financing approval, but not later than three years from the completion of the relevant investment project, (iii) any job created had to be maintained five years after its creation. The state aid scheme was available until 31 December 2023, and the grants were to be paid until 2028.

[162] Moreover, on 1 September 2022, Government Decision no. 959/2022 approved a state aid scheme for the provision of grants for investments in certain manufacturing industries. Eligible industries include the manufacturing of drinks, textiles, clothing articles, paper products, chemical products, pharmaceutical products and so on. Financing agreements were issued, based on this scheme, until 31 December 2023, in compliance with state aid legislation and the regional map authorized by the European Commission by Decision C (2021) 9750 of 20 December 2021 and approved by Government Decision no. 311/2022 regarding the maximum intensity of regional state aid in the period 2022–2027 for initial investments, within the limit of the annual budget allocated to the scheme.

[163] The payment of the state aid is made in the timeframe 2022–2027, based on the financing agreements issued, within the budget allocated to the scheme.

[164] On 13 April 2022, the implementation procedure and the state aid scheme associated with the IMM PROD Programme were approved through Ministry of Finance Order no. 955/2022.

[165] The main objective of the IMM PROD Programme is to ensure liquidity for the current activity and the financing of investments made by SMEs, including start-ups, from the urban area in order to achieve the following specific objectives:

(a) encouraging domestic production of consumer goods, increasing production capacity;
(b) reconversion from intermediation to production;
(c) digitization of the activity;
(d) aligning/improving environmental standards, including improving energy efficiency in the production processes.

[166] The SMEs may benefit from a grant of up to EUR2.3 m, subject to certain qualification criteria, such as not being in financial difficulty, as defined by applicable regulations, not being in an ongoing lawsuit with the Ministry of Finance or the partner credit institution, not being in insolvency and so on.

[167] Expenses such as acquisition of equipment, acquisition of land for production, acquisition of equipment, software, consulting services for digitalization and others are eligible within the IMM PROD Programme.

[168] Furthermore, on 7 July 2023, the national programme for the development of domestic production of construction products and materials, 'CONSTRUCTPLUS', having as its object the financial support of private investments for the establishment and/or development of production capacities for construction products and materials, has been approved through Government Emergency Ordinance no. 68/2023.

[169] The 'CONSTRUCTPLUS' Programme provides financial support for regional development and aims to:

(a) reduce the trade deficit resulting from the import of construction materials;
(b) stimulate investments in less developed countries;
(c) increase the internal production of construction products and materials.

[170] The financial aid through the 'CONSTRUCTPLUS' Programme represents regional non-reimbursable state aid of a maximum amount of EUR50 m, but not more than 75% of the investment value and without exceeding the maximum intensity of state aid provided for in the Regional Map authorised by the European

Commission by Decision C (2021) 9750 of 20 December 2021 and approved by Government Decision no. 311/2022 regarding the maximum intensity of regional state aid in the period 2022–2027 for initial investments. The Programme is multiannual for the timeframe 2023–2026.

[171] On 11 January 2024, the European Commission approved, under EU State aid rules, a EUR126 m Romanian scheme to support investments in ports facing increased trade flows after Russia's war against Ukraine.

[172] Romania notified the Commission of its plans to support companies active in certain Romanian ports to invest in additional handling or storage facilities for processing goods that deviated from their normal trading routes due to Russia's war against Ukraine and the collapse of Ukraine's direct maritime export routes. The scheme, with a budget of EUR126 m (around RON626 m), will run until 31 December 2024.

[173] Under the scheme, the aid will take the form of grants up to EUR10 m to logistics companies active in Romanian maritime and inland ports located on: (i) the eastern border of the EU (Constanţa, Galaţi, Giurgiu); (ii) the Danube – Black Sea Canal (Poarta Albă, Midia, and Năvodari); (iii) the Sulina Canal or in the 'satellite' ports of Constanţa (Midia, and Mangalia).

[174] The aid cannot exceed the lowest of the following amounts: (i) EUR10 m per beneficiary, (ii) the funding gap, or (iii) 65% of the eligible costs of the project.

[175] The measure will be partly funded through EU Cohesion funds and will contribute to the functioning of the EU-Ukraine Solidarity Lanes by facilitating the trade flows in and from Ukraine.

[176] Pursuant to the Romanian legal framework for the support of small and medium enterprises (SMEs), SMEs may benefit from various special state aid measures, including: (i) grants offered to SMEs for the payment of start-up capital; (ii) grants for investments in the production and services sector; (iii) establishment of guarantee/counter-guarantee/venture capital funds; (iv) the set-up of low-interest loan schemes; and (v) the set-up of other schemes or financial instruments, etc.

[177] There has also been recently significant support towards the energy sector, particularly given the recent wave of interest in renewable energy sources capacities ('**RES**'), especially in photovoltaic projects ('**PV**'). In the context of the European Green Deal and, more recently, of the REPowerEU Plan and of dedicated European Union funding, Romanian authorities have started shaping new RES support schemes. These would mainly include new contracts for difference support mechanism ('**CfD Mechanism**'), as well as particular support schemes financed from various sources, including Romania's National Recovery and Resilience Plan ('**NRRP**'), the EU Modernization Fund or the Just Transition Fund.

[178] *CfD Mechanism.* The Romanian government has been expressing its intention to implement a CfD Mechanism to encourage investments in low-carbon generation technologies. According to a memorandum adopted in 2020, the new mechanism would cover, among others, RES generation capacities, including PV.

[179] *NRRP*. The NRRP envisages a total number of 139 reforms and investments, which cover significant projects in six areas, including green transition, for which 41% of the total budgetary allocation is included.

[180] *The EU Modernisation Fund*. Estimated at approx. EUR13 bn, it is supporting, among others, investment proposals in the areas of electricity generation from renewable sources.

[181] *The Just Transition* Fund is targeting coal-reliant countries such as Romania, and EUR2.14 bn is expected to be directed to Romania with a view to support transition to clean energy. The funds will be allocated to six counties: Dolj, Galaţi, Gorj, Hunedoara, Mureş and Prahova.

12.5.2 Free Areas

[182] A special incentive regime applies in Romania for the so-called free zone (in Romanian, *zone libere*), namely a geographical area located in the territory of Romania, where operators carry on business and the goods, means of transportation, and other assets are subject to a special customs regime. Currently, Romania has seven free zone areas (Braila, Galati, Constanta-Sud, Basarabi, Sulina, Giurgiu and Arad-Curtici), being generally located near the Romanian state's border.

[183] The free zones lost much of their appeal after the accession of Romania to the EU and the cancellation of their favourable tax regime. However, investors in free zones still benefit from certain incentives, which may still render these areas attractive for investment. For example, with respect to investments made in the free zones, foreign or domestic investors benefit, among other things, from grants amounting to: (i) 50% of the value of the eligible costs of investments made by large enterprises; and (ii) 65% of the value of the eligible costs in the case of SMEs.

12.5.3 Industrial Parks

[184] Buildings, constructions and land located in industrial parks and technology parks are exempt from local taxes on property.

[185] There are several other benefits granted for the development of a business in an industrial park, such as: (i) local tax exemptions and/or tax cuts for immovable assets and land related to the industrial park; (ii) incentives granted by the local tax authorities; (iii) development of programmes for infrastructure, investment and equipment endowments granted by public authorities and foreign financial assistance; and (iv) concessions and structural development funds.

[186] In addition, entities located in industrial parks may benefit from various services provided by the park manager free of charge or from reduced fees and favourable conditions for the use of the park's infrastructure.

[187] Other fiscal incentives that should be taken into account by foreign investors in Romania include the following.

12.5.4 Tax Exemption in the Case of Dividends Paid by a Romanian Legal Entity

[188] This exemption is applicable in cases where the income beneficiary fulfils the following conditions:

(1) It is a legal entity resident in the EU.
(2) It pays a profit tax or a similar tax.
(3) It holds at least 10% of the registered capital of the undertaking, which is a Romanian legal entity, for an uninterrupted period of at least one year ending on the date of payment of the dividend.

For this exemption to be applied, the non-resident beneficiary must provide at the date of payment a valid tax residency certificate and the beneficial owner statement.

The exemption was included in the Romanian tax legislation as an effect of the transposition of the EU Parent-Subsidiary Directive.

12.5.5 Tax Exemption in the Case of Interest and Royalties Paid by a Romanian Legal Entity

[189] This exemption is applicable in cases where the income beneficiary and the income payer are associated companies resident in the EU (for a period of a minimum of two years).

[190] A company is an '*associated company*' of a second company if, at least:

(1) the first company has a direct minimum holding of 25% in the capital of the second company; or
(2) the second company has a direct minimum holding of 25% in the capital of the first company; or
(3) a third company has a direct minimum holding of 25% both in the capital of the first company and in the capital of the second company.

For this exemption to be applied, the non-resident beneficiary must provide at the date of payment a valid tax residency certificate and the beneficial owner statement.

The exemption was included in the Romanian tax legislation as an effect of the transposition of the EU Interest-Royalty Directive.

12.5.6 Tax Exemptions in Favour of Holdings

[191] The Fiscal Code provides for certain types of income which are not taxable for Corporate Income Tax (CIT) purposes, such as:

(1) dividends;
(2) income from the evaluation/revaluation/sale/assignment of participation titles;

(3) income from the liquidation of a legal entity – a Romanian legal entity or a legal entity that is resident in a country with which Romania has concluded a Double Tax Treaty).

[192] The above reliefs are applicable only if at least 10% of the share capital has been held for an interrupted period of at least one year, except for dividends paid by a Romanian legal entity to another Romanian legal entity, which are not taxable for CIT purposes with no additional requirement. For the dividends received from foreign legal entities, there is an additional condition stipulating that the entity distributing the dividends pays profit tax or a similar tax (i.e., legal entities applying the microenterprise tax regime).

[193] However, the following tax incentives that are applicable to both foreign and local investors should also be observed.

12.5.7 Exemption for Reinvested Profit

[194] Profit taxpayers in Romania who invest in eligible equipment, IT software/ the right to use IT software, assets used in the production and processing activities, as well as those representing a technological upgrade, will benefit from a tax exemption of the reinvested profit.

[195] In order to benefit from this incentive, the equipment must be kept for at least half its normal useful economic life in accordance with the applicable accounting rules, but for no more than five years. The companies benefiting from this incentive cannot use the accelerated depreciation method for these assets.

12.5.8 Deductions for Research and Development Expenses

[196] For research and development activities, an additional deduction in the calculation of taxable profit is granted, amounting to 50% of the eligible expenses of these activities. The additional deduction must be calculated on a quarterly/annual basis. If a tax loss is realized, this must be recovered as provided for by the Fiscal Code.

[197] Furthermore, accelerated depreciation for devices and equipment used in the research and development activities may be applied.

[198] In addition, the newly incorporated taxpayers that perform exclusively innovation, research and development activities, as defined by Government Ordinance 57/2002 regarding scientific research and technological development, as amended, as well as the related activities, are exempt from CIT for the first ten years of activity. In the case of taxpayers already incorporated at the date when this provision entered into force (i.e., 24 July 2017), the CIT exemption is applicable for a period of ten years starting with this date (i.e., 24 July 2017). State aid regulations must be observed/followed in order to apply for this incentive.

12.5.9 Accelerated Amortization Method

[199] The Romanian Fiscal Code entitles taxpayers to apply the accelerated depreciation method in case of acquisition of various items of machinery and equipment, pursuant to which a maximum of 50% of the fiscal value of the asset is tax-deductible during the first year of usage, while the remaining value of the asset may be depreciated over its remaining useful life through the straight-line method.

12.5.10 Guarantees Against Expropriation or Nationalization

[200] The Romanian Constitution guarantees private property, irrespective of the nature of its ownership and restricts any expropriation measures unless the expropriation is performed on the grounds of public utility and subject always to fair compensation being paid in advance to the expropriated individual or entity.

[201] Nationalization, or any other measures of forced transfer into public ownership based on social, ethical, religious, political or other discriminatory criteria with respect to the titleholder, are also restricted pursuant to the Romanian Constitution.

[202] These guarantees against expropriation and nationalization established in the Romanian Constitution are also stated in the Romanian Civil Code.

[203] However, exceptional measures are allowed only if the following conditions are cumulatively fulfilled: (a) the measure is taken on grounds of public utility; (b) the measure is non-discriminatory; (c) the measure is taken pursuant to the law; and (d) the measure is taken only subject to the payment of prior, fair and effective compensation.

[204] Romania is also party to the Convention on the Settlement of Investment Disputes between States and Nationals of other States (ICSID Convention) and has ratified over seventy bilateral investment treaties (BITs), each of which treaties provide supplementary guarantees against expropriation, nationalization and measures with equivalent effect to investors from states which have entered into BITs with Romania.

[205] Mechanisms/safeguards allowing for the payment of dividends abroad and repatriation of profits and/or the proceeds of liquidation or sale.

[206] As a general rule, dividends paid to non-residents are subject to a 16% withholding tax unless the more favourable provisions of a double tax treaty apply. Romania has entered into more than eighty double tax treaties pursuant to which non-residents from countries which are party to a double tax treaty with Romania may benefit from more favourable taxation rates stipulated in the applicable double tax treaty if such is the case.

[207] Moreover, Romania has fully implemented the provisions of the EU Parent-Subsidiary Directive, pursuant to which dividends distributed by Romanian companies to companies resident in an EU or EEA Member State are exempt from withholding tax if the recipient company has held, at the time of distribution, a

minimum of 10% of the shares of the Romanian company for a continuous period of at least one year.

[208] In order to benefit from the EU Parent-Subsidiary Directive, non-residents must present a tax residency certificate and an affidavit attesting compliance with the mandatory requirements provided by the EU Parent-Subsidiary Directive.

[209] Pursuant to Romanian fiscal law, the proceeds arising from the liquidation of Romanian legal entities are deemed to be generated in Romania and are generally subject to the 16% corporate tax applicable to the taxable profits resulting from liquidation, i.e., the difference between the proceeds realized and the expenses incurred for the purpose of realizing the proceeds, computed as at the beginning of the fiscal year.

[210] However, with effect from 2014, the proceeds from the liquidation of a Romanian legal entity or of a foreign legal entity resident in a state which has entered into a double tax treaty with Romania are exempt from Romanian corporate tax if the recipient company has held, at the time of the initiation of the liquidation proceedings, a minimum of 10% of the shares of the legal entity subject to liquidation for a continuous period of at least one year. This exemption applies only in cases where the beneficiary of the revenues is a Romanian legal entity. In other cases, the profit generated from the liquidation is subject to tax in Romania at the flat rate of 16%, which will be withheld by the legal person before the liquidation becomes effective.

[211] As a general rule, profits from the sale of shares held in Romanian companies are subject to a tax of 16% regardless of the fiscal residence or the legal personality of the vendor. With effect from 2014, the revenues are not taxable in cases where the vendor is a legal entity resident in Romania or in a country with which Romania has concluded a Double Tax Treaty holding at least 10% in the share capital for a period of at least one year.

[212] Also, the profits generated from the sale or use of immovable assets located in Romania are subject to the 16% corporate tax.

[213] Safeguards for the payment of interest on foreign loans or payment of fees and charges to foreign companies for Intellectual property (IP) or technology transfer.

[214] Interest paid in relation to a foreign loan, as well as royalties, is generally subject to 16% withholding taxes unless the more favourable provisions of a double tax treaty apply.

[215] Romania has fully implemented the Interest and Royalties Directive, pursuant to which interest paid by a Romanian company to a company resident in another EU Member State is exempt from withholding tax provided that one of the companies held at least 25% of the share capital of the other company involved in the transaction, or a third company held at least 25% of the share capital of each company for a continuous period of at least two years.

[216] For the purpose of benefiting from the Interest and Royalties Directive, non-residents must present a tax residency certificate and an affidavit attesting compliance with the mandatory requirements provided by the Interest and Royalties Directive.

[217] In Romania, there are various types of local financing options for acquisition, consisting mainly of bank loans, syndicated loans, leveraged buyouts or other similar types of financing transactions. Nevertheless, after the onset of the financial crisis in 2008, local banks became reluctant to grant local financing for acquisitions, and even if they were disposed to provide such financing solutions, a syndicated structure was preferred for mitigating exposure risks to the maximum extent.

[218] A foreign lender is allowed to take security over local immovable property, as there are no interdictions in this respect under Romanian law.

[219] There are no controls over the transfer of funds to foreign lenders for the payment of interest or the repayment of capital. Residents borrowing from foreign lenders for a period greater than one year are nevertheless obliged for statistical purposes to notify the relevant loans to the NBR. In respect of the interest payable to a foreign lender, it is important to mention that, according to the Romanian Fiscal Code, such payments are taxable in Romania unless a double taxation treaty between Romania and the country of the foreign lender is in force and provides otherwise.

[220] According to Regulation no. 4/2005 issued by the NBR, a local/domestic company is entitled to hold bank accounts in foreign countries.

[221] There are no exchange control or currency regulations currently in force in Romania, which might affect foreign investors.

12.6 Specific Issues of Company/Securities Law

12.6.1 Shareholder Approval

[222] Entering into M&A transactions is subject to the specific restrictions set out in the constitutive act of the company and more generally in the Companies Act.

[223] There are no specific rules for the approval of the merger or spin-off by the shareholders. Thus, in case of a limited liability company, the general meeting shall decide by a vote representing an absolute majority of the members and of the shares unless the articles of association provide otherwise. The merger or spin-off of a joint-stock company must be approved by the extraordinary general meeting of the shareholders (the level of quorums and the majority of votes being as detailed above).

[224] In addition, the shareholders of a joint-stock company have to grant their approval for any M&A transaction involving the sale, acquisition, lease, exchange or grant of guarantees related to any assets of the company in cases where the value of such assets exceeds half of the total book value of all the assets of the company.

This obligation is not mandatory for limited liability companies unless such shareholders' approval has been provided for in the company's constitutive act. As a matter of practice, significant M&A transactions involving limited liability companies are also approved by the shareholders.

[225] Also, for listed companies, the acquisition, sale, exchange or grant of guarantees involving immoveable assets, the value of which exceed, either individually or cumulatively, during a financial year, 20% of the total immoveable assets, less any debts, must be approved in advance by the shareholders. This same rule applies to any leasing transaction for a period in excess of one year involving tangible assets whose individual or cumulative value against the same co-contractor or persons involved or acting in concert exceeds 20% of the total value of tangible assets less any claims on the date when the legal document is concluded, as well as any associations for a period of time longer than one year which exceed the aforementioned value.

12.6.2 Directors' Duties

[226] Romanian law does not provide for any specific duties of directors and managers towards the shareholders of the company in relation to M&A transactions, except for those duties related to the merger and spin-off process where directors play a more important part, for example: (i) to prepare the merger/spin-off project; (ii) to prepare a report on the merger/spin-off process; and (iii) to make available to the shareholders of participating companies documents regarding the relevant restructuring process (e.g., financial statements of the companies for the previous three years).

[227] However, the general duties of directors do apply in cases where they are engaged in an M&A transaction, such as the duty to abstain from voting on any transaction in which the director holds an interest contrary to the company's interest; the duty to enforce the decisions of the general meeting of shareholders and to carry out their functions in accordance with the best interests of the company and with appropriate diligence and prudence.

12.6.3 Form of Consideration

[228] Under the Company Law, at the time of incorporation, contributions to a joint-stock company's share capital may be made in cash, in kind (e.g., assets) and in receivables. In the case of limited liability companies only, contributions in cash and in kind to the share capital are allowed. For both joint-stock companies and limited liability companies, cash contribution is mandatory upon the setting up of the company.

[229] Irrespective of the type of company, shares cannot be issued against a contribution to services to be performed by the shareholders.

[230] Shareholders contributing receivables to a joint-stock company's share capital will not be discharged from liability towards the company until the actual receipt of the related payment. If payment cannot be obtained, then the contributing shareholder is liable for the amount representing the value of the receivables increased by the legal interest rate as of the date of maturity of the relevant receivables.

[231] In the case of a share capital increase, only contributions in cash and/or in kind are allowed, while contributions in receivables are generally forbidden. However, shareholders are entitled to convert their debts held against the company into shares.

[232] Certain formalities are required in the case of contributions in kind, as follows:

(1) generally, for contributions in kind to the share capital of a joint-stock company (either in the context of incorporation of the company or in the context of a subsequent share capital increase), a formal evaluation report will need to be performed by one or more independent experts appointed by the commercial registry; and
(2) for contributions in kind of immovable assets (e.g., real estate properties), irrespective of whether the company is a joint-stock company or a limited liability company, relevant documents approving the incorporation/share capital increase (i.e., constitutive act or shareholder(s) resolution, as the case may be) will need to be concluded in notarized form.

[233] After the shares are issued against a non-cash consideration, there are no subsequent restrictions on the disposal of such shares.

12.6.4 Financial Assistance

[234] According to the Romanian companies law, it is unlawful for a joint-stock company (*Romanian: societate pe acŢiuni*) to give, whether by means of a loan, guarantee, security or otherwise, any financial assistance for the purchase of or subscription of its own shares by a third party (such as the acquiring company). The prohibition does not apply (i) to credit or financial institutions in relation to transactions carried out in their ordinary course of business or (ii) to transactions made for the purchase of shares by/for the employees of the company, provided such transaction does not result in a reduction of the company's net assets below the aggregate of the company's share capital and statutory reserves (as dictated by the law or the company's by-laws). Although the legislation only refers to financial assistance provided by the target, in the absence of relevant case law, the prudent approach is also to avoid the provision of such assistance by Romanian subsidiaries of the target.

[235] The prohibition is generally accepted not to apply to limited liability companies (*Romanian: societăŢi cu răspundere limitată*), as the legislation does not expressly provide that the prohibition applies to limited liability companies as well.

[236] Also, unlike other jurisdictions, there is no 'whitewash procedure' or other equivalent exemptions regulated under Romanian law.

12.6.5 Security Interests

[237] In cases where an acquisition is being financed by bank loans, there are multiple types of security available for securing the respective bank loans, such as: (i) immovable hypothec over the immovable assets of the borrower; (ii) movable hypothec over movable assets of the borrower (including receivables, insurance policies, IP, equipment, vehicles, raw materials and stocks, natural resources, crops to be harvest, forests to be cut, and any other tangible or intangible movable assets); (iii) movable hypothec over the bank accounts opened by the borrower with Romanian credit institutions; (iv) movable hypothec over the shares and related rights in the borrower; and (v) movable hypothec over the universality of movable assets.

[238] Generally, the concept of a floating charge over all assets does not exist in Romania. According to Romanian legislation, security agreements must comprise a description of the hypothecated asset, which is sufficiently accurate and which reasonably allows its identification. By way of exception, creditors may also take security over a universality of assets, whose nature and content must be expressly described in the relevant security agreement. This type of security is very similar to a floating charge; however, the assets over which enforcement is to be conducted may be determined only when enforcement is initiated, as the specific assets comprising the universality are not identified or 'crystallized' before that moment.

[239] It is mandatory for any security agreements referred to under limbs (ii) to (iv) above to be registered with the National Registry for Security Interest (the '*Registry*') in order for them to be opposable against third parties. Also, the rank of the security is given by the order of registration with the Registry. In case of the bank accounts hypothec agreement, it is recommended that, in addition to the registration with the Registry, lenders obtain control over the bank accounts held with the relevant banks in order to ensure that their claim is preferred in an enforcement scenario.

[240] Security over immovable assets must be registered with the relevant land book registry held at the location of the respective immovable assets. Currently, such registration is required as a means of ensuring enforceability against third parties; however, once all land cadastral registration has been completed in Romania, the registration with land book registries will be required for the very validity of immovable hypothec agreements (in addition to the normal opposability ensured through the publication of the security in land registries).

[241] The enforcement of a security in Romania is generally easy/practicable, although quite time-consuming in practice, with an enforcement officer and a judicial court being typically involved. The enforcement procedure for security over immovable assets is provided under the Romanian Civil Procedure Code and is mandatory, while creditors seeking enforcement over movable assets are entitled to choose between the general enforcement procedure provided by the Romanian Civil Procedure Code and a special enforcement procedure provided by the Romanian Civil Code (which is essentially more flexible, quicker and aims at ensuring a swift and peaceful realization of the security with as little intervention of judicial organs as possible). In the particular case of the movable hypothec over shares in Romanian companies, the relevant case law is quite insufficient as the enforcement of such type of security has not sufficiently been tested in practice. Under all circumstances, a special, non-contentious procedure is required to be followed for the obtaining of the enforcement authorization (*Romanian: încuviintarea executarii silite*) before the enforcement itself is started.

[242] In an insolvency scenario, as a rule, there are no preferential creditors which will rank ahead of secured creditors (irrespective of whether their claims have arisen during, before or after the insolvency has been initiated; please note, however, that secured creditors having claims created during the insolvency period are preferred to all other secured creditors). As an exception, the judicial receiver and the liquidator involved in the insolvency proceedings have to be paid first from the amounts recovered through the sale of the secured assets, which will also cover, as a matter of priority, the taxes and other expenses related to the relevant sale, as well as the receivables of the utility providers created subsequent to the opening of the insolvency proceedings, as provided by the law.

[243] According to the current insolvency legislation, all fraudulent acts concluded by the debtor in the last two years before the commencement of the insolvency procedure may be declared null and void by a judge (such as the free transfer of assets, acts concluded with all parties' intention to hide assets from creditors' pursuit or to hinder their rights by any means). This general period of two years prior to the insolvency procedure is also known as the 'suspect period'. Also, in some specific cases, shorter periods are provided (such as operations in which the debtor's performance openly exceeds its consideration or anticipated debt repayments initially scheduled to be due at a date falling after the commencement of insolvency proceedings are challengeable if occurring six months prior to insolvency).

12.6.6 Completion Formalities

Transferability of Shares in a Joint-Stock Company

[244] Under Romanian law, the shares issued by a joint-stock company may be issued as registered shares (in both material and dematerialized form). The type of shares issued by a joint-stock company impacts the method of transfer thereof. Thus, (i) registered shares issued in dematerialized form are transferred by registration in the shareholders' registry (by means of a statement registered in the shareholders' register of the company signed by the assignor and the assignee or by their representatives); and (ii) registered shares issued in material form are transferred by registration in the shareholders' registry (as in the case of shares issued in dematerialized form) together with the endorsement of the share certificates by the assignor and the assignee or by their representatives.

[245] In the case of a joint-stock company, the transfer of shares to third parties does not require any formal approval of the other shareholders unless otherwise stated in the constitutive act of the company. Also, it is not mandatory for such transfers to be registered with the commercial registry. However, registration with the commercial registry is advisable in order to ensure enforceability against third parties.

Transferability of Shares in a Limited Liability Company

[246] The transfer of shares in the case of a limited liability company to persons outside the company may only be carried out with the approval of the shareholders representing at least three-quarters of the company's share capital unless a different majority is set forth in the articles of association of the company.

[247] The transfer of shares must be registered with the commercial registry and in the shareholders' register of the company.

[248] The transfer of shares shall be effective between the shareholders and the company from the date of resolution of the GSM approving the transfer and between the seller and the purchaser from the date of the share purchase agreement.

12.6.7 Transfer of Immovable Properties

[249] All transfers of immovable properties shall be registered with the relevant Land Book Office in order to ensure enforceability against third parties. The registration shall be performed on the basis of the documents attesting to the transfer of ownership right. Also, under Romanian law, all documents attesting to the transfer of ownership over land shall be concluded in the authenticated form before a public notary. In such a case, a transaction structured as an asset deal which involves the transfer of ownership over immovable goods (e.g., land and buildings) will need to be concluded in authentic form.

[250] In case of a transaction structured as a share deal, even if the target company owns certain immovable goods, no authentication is needed given that direct ownership over the relevant plots of land does not change (i.e., the relevant plots of land will remain the property of the target company).

[251] However, if the change of ownership over immovable assets (e.g., land and buildings) is the result of a merger, certain documents of the merger process need to be concluded in authentic form (e.g., the merger project, the GSM resolution approving the merger project).

[252] On a case-by-case basis, other formalities/procedures could be necessary depending on the structure of the transaction and industry of the target company, such as:

(1) the approval of the Competition Council (from both a merger control and national security perspective);
(2) formalities with the State Office for Inventions and Trademarks, for transfer of IP rights;
(3) formalities with the National Bank of Romania;
(4) formalities with the FSA;

(5) formalities with fiscal authorities (e.g., registration of the change of ownership over vehicles, buildings, lands or other assets); and
(6) formalities with labour authorities.

12.6.8 Costs and Fees

[253] Generally, transactions imply a variable number of steps, which depend on the value and industry of the transaction as well as on the assets to be transferred. As an overview of possible costs, fees, notifications, announcements, filings or completion certificates triggered/necessary in an M&A transaction, at least the following should be considered:

(1) *Costs and fees*: Land Book fees are required at registering transfer of immovable ownership (e.g., mergers or spin-offs, ownership or dismemberments over immovable properties), notary fees (e.g., authentication of acts and corporate documents, sale–purchase agreements), fiscal fees (e.g., VAT, income tax on transfer of shares), authorities fees (e.g., State Office for Inventions and Trademarks for transmission of trademark as a result of a merger, Commercial Registry fees on registration of corporate approvals or merger/spin-off projects).
(2) *Filings/notifications/announcements*: public bodies that could require notifications or regulatory approvals during the M&A process would be: the RCC; the National Bank of Romania for acquisitions of qualifying participations in the banking sector, the Romanian FSA for acquisitions of qualifying participations in the securities and insurance sectors; the Territorial Labour Inspectorate in case of transfer of employees; the Romanian Top Level Domain; corporate approvals, merger or spin-off projects will need to be submitted to the Commercial Registry; the transfer of employees in case of mergers or business transfers should be registered in the Employees Electronic Register.
(3) *Completion certificates*: registration certificate would be issued by the Commercial Registry (e.g., in mergers or spin-offs, in a transfer of shares transaction), Competition Council clearance decision; non-objection decisions by the National Bank of Romania or the Romanian FSA in the relevant regulated sectors.

12.6.9 Dividends

[254] The Romanian corporate and fiscal legal framework provides the same fiscal treatment for foreign investors as in the case of Romanian investors, guarantees free access to domestic markets and allows foreign investors to participate in privatizations. There is no limit on foreign participation in commercial enterprises. Foreign investors are entitled to establish fully owned enterprises in Romania (although joint ventures are more typical) and to convert and repatriate 100% of after-tax profits.

[255] Under the Company Law, dividends are the pro rata portion of the profits to be paid to each shareholder only from determined profits. Given that accommodation and fostering of investments is one of the major goals in the legal framework drafting process, no express restrictions on the payment of dividends are conditioned upon whether the dividends are to be paid to a domestic or to a foreign shareholder.

[256] Unless otherwise provided in the constitutive act, dividends are paid to the shareholder(s) proportionally to their contribution to the paid-in share capital. Until July 2018, the distribution of the dividends was made on a date agreed upon by the shareholders but no later than six months from the date of approval of the annual financial statements of the previous year. Otherwise, the company must pay a penalty for the delay in payment.

[257] As of July 2018, a law has entered into force that amended the currently existing legislation in order to allow the distribution of interim dividends on a quarterly basis. Prior to the enactment of such changes, the distribution of dividends was possible only after the approval of the annual financial statements. In other words, the distribution of interim dividends was not allowed. Pursuant to these changes, the distribution of dividends to shareholders is possible on a quarterly basis, provided that the following conditions are met: (i) the company has prepared interim financial statements; and (ii) the shareholders approved through a resolution of the GSM the distribution of interim dividends.

[258] The dividends that can be distributed on these interim financial statements are limited to: (i) the net accounting profit registered by the company during that period plus the reported profits and the sums available in the reserves for that purpose and (ii) deducting any losses carried out forward and the legal and statutory reserves (as detailed below).

[259] Such interim dividends would then be adjusted based on the annual financial statements, and the amounts distributed as interim dividends exceeding the dividends which can be distributed as per the annual financial statements would need to be reimbursed to the company within sixty days of the date when the annual financial statements were approved.

[260] In the event dividends are wrongfully paid, shareholders are under an obligation to repay the relevant amounts if the company can prove that the shareholders knew or should have known that the dividends were wrongfully paid. Such claim may be filed by the company before a court of law within a maximum of three years from their distribution.

[261] *Reserve fund.* As regards the value of the profit to be distributed to the shareholders, at least 5% of the company's profits must be set aside each year until it reaches a minimum of 20% of the share capital for the purpose of establishing a reserve fund. If, for any reason, the reserve fund is reduced under this threshold, it has to be reconstituted from yearly profits.

[262] Also, any profit obtained from a sale of shares of the company for a price exceeding their nominal value must also be included in the reserve fund, provided that such profit is not used for payment of the expenses of issue or for purposes of their amortization.

12.6.10 Purchase of Own Shares

[263] Under the Company Law, a joint-stock company cannot subscribe to its own shares. If shares are subscribed through persons acting in their own name but on behalf of the company, it is considered that the buyer subscribed the shares on its own behalf and may be held liable for the related price thereof.

[264] A joint-stock company is entitled to acquire its own shares, either directly or through an intermediary acting on its own behalf, only by observing the following conditions:

(1) the extraordinary general meeting of the joint-stock company authorizing the acquisition has to establish the method of acquisition, the maximum number of shares to be acquired, the minimum and maximum value thereof and the period for carrying out the operation, which cannot exceed eighteen months from the date of registration with the Commercial Registry and the related value thereof;
(2) the nominal value of the shares acquired by the company, including those already in its portfolio, cannot exceed 10% of the subscribed share capital;
(3) only fully cleared shares may be acquired; and
(4) the acquired shares may only be paid from profits available for distribution and from the available reserves of the company, except for the legal reserves, amounts registered in the last approved annual financial statement.

[265] However, if the shares are acquired for the purpose of transferring these shares to the employees of the company, such transfer will need to take place within a maximum of twelve months from the acquisition date.

[266] The above restraints on the acquisition by a company of its own shares do not apply in cases where the acquisition by a company of a certain number of its own shares, fully cleared, takes place in one of the following situations:

(1) for the purpose of reducing the share capital by cancelling a number of own shares as approved by the GSM;
(2) due to the effect of a universal transfer;
(3) fully cleared shares, acquired through a court decision on enforcement over a shareholder also acting as debtor of the company; and
(4) with free title.

[267] In the event that a company breaches these conditions in acquiring its own shares, the relevant shares must be transferred within, at most, one year from the date of their subscription. If the nominal value of the shares acquired by the company through one of the scenarios at points (ii)–(iv) above, including the value of its own shares previously acquired, exceeds 10% of the share capital, the shares exceeding such percentage have to be sold within three years from their acquisition. If the company fails to sell the shares as previously described herein, the company will be under an obligation to reduce its share capital to that end.

[268] The shares acquired pursuant to the conditions described above do not entitle their holders to any dividends during the period of time they are in the possession of the company. The voting rights attached to such shares are also suspended.

[269] As regards repatriation of the proceeds obtained during such acquisition process, they could be freely repatriated to a foreign owner, provided that the relevant Romanian tax obligations on payment of the profits/income are observed.

12.6.11 The Corporate Veil

[270] The Civil Code allows a claimant, under certain strict circumstances, to try to 'pierce the corporate veil' and directly pursue a parent company for the obligations and liabilities of its subsidiary. In the following cases, the Romanian courts may be willing to pierce the corporate veil (however, such cases are rare in practice and are seen more as being theoretical):

(1) if an interested person proves that the acts/activities of the parent amount to a fraud of or abuse of the subsidiary's patrimony or breach the public interest; and
(2) if the interested person is able to prove its good faith.

[271] The possibility of piercing the corporate veil is also regulated by the Company Law under limited conditions: a shareholder who abuses the company's limited liability as a legal entity will be held liable for the due debts of the company if its actions are considered by a court of law as representing a fraud on the rights of the company's creditors. For example, a shareholder could be considered as abusing the company's limited liability and be held liable to an unlimited extent when it disposes of the company's assets in its own interest or for a third party's benefit, knowing (or if it should have known) that the company will not be in a position to honour its debts as a result of such actions.

12.6.12 Insolvency

[272] According to Romanian legislation, a person is entitled to purchase shares in an insolvent company only if: (a) the insolvent company is in a reorganization procedure; and (b) the reorganization plan expressly provides for the possibility to sell shares in that company. If the court considers that a reorganization procedure is not useful for the company, thus not allowing it, the purchase of shares will not be possible. Therefore, a person cannot purchase a company that is in liquidation. As for a company in receivership, there are two situations: (i) a company that is in receivership but also in a reorganization procedure can be sold to a third party, while (ii) a company that is in receivership but not in a reorganization procedure cannot be sold to a third party.

[273] Some of the main implications of buying shares or businesses which have gone into insolvency are as follows: (a) the buyer will have to observe and follow the reorganization plan which has been voted for and also to conduct its activity under the strict supervision of a judicial receiver; (b) there is a risk that the reorganization plan may fail, in which case the liquidation procedure will come into effect; (c) when buying an insolvent company, the buyer acquires all the receivables, but also all the debts of that company.

12.6.13 Choice of Law

[274] Choice of law, jurisdiction and arbitration clauses are generally recognized and enforceable in Romania. The choice of law should, however, be correlated with the jurisdiction clause. For example, if Romanian courts or arbitration in Romania is chosen as the preferred dispute resolution venue, it is advisable that the governing law of the transaction be Romanian law as well, with which Romanian courts or arbitration tribunals are obviously fully familiar.

12.7 Specific Rules on Public Takeovers

[275] Public takeovers are supervised by the Romanian FSA. The Capital Markets Law no. 297/2004, Law no. 24/2017 on issuers of financial instruments and market operations, the Romanian FSA Regulation no. 5/2018 regarding issuers of financial instruments and market operations and further guidelines/regulations issued by the Romanian FSA all set out the relevant rules under which public takeovers may be implemented in Romania.

[276] The public takeover rules apply to joint-stock companies listed on the BSE and those traded via an ATS (i.e., AeRo).

[277] The rules governing mandatory takeovers do not apply to issuers traded via an ATS (i.e., AeRo).

[278] The following types of public purchases are implemented in the Romanian market:

(a) public purchase offers targeting a portion of the shareholdings in an issuer, in the context in which the offeror is already a shareholder of the issuer and it has a holding above 33% or below these thresholds, but it is not targeting a participation above 33%;
(b) public purchase offers targeting all the shares in an issuer in the context in which the offeror is already a shareholder of the issuer and has a holding above 33%;

(c) voluntary takeover targeting all the shares in an issuer, in the context in which the offeror does not own any shares in the issuer or owns a participation below 33% and is targeting the acquisition of more than a 33% stake in the issuer; and
(d) mandatory takeover imposed by the relevant regulations following the acquisition of a 33% stake by the offeror, as the case may be, in order for the offeror to take over all the remaining shares in the issuer.

[279] In each case, the relevant offer must be addressed to all shareholders of the relevant issuer.

[280] There are no specific advantages or disadvantages concerning the above structures. In other words, these structures are imposed by the applicable regulations and driven by the relevant context in which the offeror is placed towards the issuer. Voluntary takeovers represent the means of taking control over an issuer in the event the number of shareholders in the issuer is very granulated and/or where any negotiations with a significant shareholder of the issuer have failed, and the implementation of the transaction via the Deal Market became impossible. In other words, if the offeror does not close the deal with a majority/controlling shareholding via the Deal Market, it will have no other choice but to initiate a public takeover to this end. Even if the transaction is implemented via the Deal Market (not based on the public purchase/takeover rules), to the extent the subscriptions reach 33%, as the case may be, the route of the mandatory takeover will need to be taken forward by the offeror.

12.8 Responsibilities of the Directors of a Target Board on Receiving an Offer

[281] Specific responsibilities arise for the directors of a target's board in the context of a voluntary takeover. To that end, the board of directors of the target has the following responsibilities:

(a) to provide the Romanian FSA, the offeror and the BSE with the board's position/opinion regarding the opportunity of the takeover;
(b) to inform the employees of the takeover and the board's position on the opportunity of the takeover;
(c) to convene the general meeting of the shareholders in order to discuss the board's position/opinion on the opportunity of the takeover in the event a significant shareholder submits a request for the relevant calling of the general meeting;
(d) from the date of receipt of the preliminary announcement until the date of completion of the voluntary takeover, to inform the Romanian FSA and the BSE of any operation that has been implemented by the board in relation to the relevant securities; and

(e) from the date of receipt of the preliminary announcement, not to enter into any agreement/arrangement or take any measures which may affect the financial standing of the target (such measure could be share capital increases, granting security over or selling assets of the target which represent one-third of the net assets in accordance with the latest financial statement of the target) or the relevant scope of the takeover (with the exception of those activities which are required in the ordinary course of business).

[282] Notwithstanding the relevant limitations set out above, the following actions may be carried out: any operation specifically approved by the extraordinary general meeting of the shareholders convened after the publication of the preliminary announcement, including operations derived from previously adopted resolutions of a company.

[283] Protective actions that could be taken after the takeover becomes public are not expressly regulated. Nevertheless, when implementing protective actions, the board must take into account that it has a loyalty obligation towards the target and must act in the best interests of the target.

[284] The following actions could be implemented in practice:

(a) the board may provide a negative opinion on the takeover (which may also be backed up by a resolution of the general meeting of the shareholders of the target);
(b) forming a blocking majority/minority within the general meeting of the shareholders;
(c) delaying implementation of the effective change of control;
(d) another investor may be sought to launch a competing offer for the same shares and with a higher price; or
(e) the launch of a purchase offer for the shares of the offeror provided that the offeror is a publicly traded company.

[285] When issuing the board's opinion or taking protective actions with regard to the takeover, the board members will have to be guided by their duties as directors. Advising the shareholders in a manner that does not respect their best interests may result in civil liability of the directors concerned for any damages incurred. In addition, to the extent such wrong advice may be intentional, the directors may also be criminally liable.

12.9 Partial Offers

[286] Offers must be addressed to all shareholders of the target and on terms which do not discriminate in any way between shareholders. The public purchase offer may target a portion of the share capital of the target.

12.10 Mandatory Bids

[287] A mandatory takeover will need to be carried out if a person, alone or acting in concert with other persons, acquires more than 33% of the voting rights of the target. A mandatory takeover needs to be launched as soon as possible, but not later than two months from the date the 33% threshold has been reached.

[288] The requirement to carry out a mandatory takeover is not applicable in circumstances where the 33% threshold had been reached by way of an exempt transaction.

[289] Exempt transactions are those through which the regulated threshold has been obtained:

(1) in the context of a privatization process;
(2) by acquiring shares from the Ministry of Public Finance or other entities legally acting within the budget receivables sector;
(3) by way of transfer between a mother company and its subsidiaries or vice versa; or
(4) by way of a voluntary takeover addressed to all shareholders and for all the shares they hold.

[290] If the 33% threshold is acquired unintentionally, within three months from the relevant reference date, a choice must be made between: (a) carrying out a mandatory takeover offer; and (b) selling the relevant shares.

[291] Unintentional transactions include the following scenarios:

(1) reduction of the share capital of the target when the target re-purchases its own shares, which are subsequently cancelled;
(2) after exercising a preference right, subscription or conversion right with respect to the initially attributed rights or the conversion of preferential shares into ordinary shares; or
(3) merger/demerger or succession.

12.11 Purchase of Shares in Advance of or During a Bid

[292] The offeror may purchase shares in the target in advance of announcing a takeover offer.

[293] Should the offeror acquire voting rights exceeding the 33% threshold of the total voting rights of the target, it must launch a mandatory takeover offer for all the remaining shares of the target within two months from the date the 33% threshold has been acquired. From the date the 33% threshold has been acquired until the closing of the mandatory takeover, the voting rights of the offeror exceeding

the 33% threshold are suspended, and the offeror is not permitted to purchase by any other means shares in the target.

[294] In the event the offeror or any persons with whom the offeror acts in concert acquires shares of the same type that are subject to the public purchase offer or the public takeover after the relevant offer is launched, outside the already pending offer, the offeror is required to increase the offer price within the pending offer to a level equal with the highest price paid by the offeror (or by any persons acting in concert with it) outside the offer. To this end, the offeror is required to file with the Romanian FSA the amendment to the offer regarding the purchase price and the number of shares subject to the offer.

[295] In order to acquire shares of the same type as those that are subject to a pending offer, the offeror or any persons with whom the offeror acts in concert must comply with the following conditions: (i) the purchase must be carried out at a higher price than that comprised within the pending offer; and (ii) the purchase must be implemented at least four business days in advance of the closing date of the pending offer.

12.12 Stakebuilding and Disclosure Obligations

[296] A person who, following share acquisition or sale transactions as well as any other operations, reaches, exceeds or decreases below the thresholds of 5%, 10%, 15%, 20%, 25%, 33%, 50% and 75% of the total voting rights must notify the Romanian FSA, the regulated market and the target within four business days from the day following the date when the relevant person becomes aware of the reaching, exceeding or decreasing below the applicable thresholds.

[297] In order for these thresholds to be calculated, the issuer must make public the total number of the issued shares and the voting rights attached to them at the end of every calendar month if, during the relevant month, a decrease or an increase in the share capital/voting rights occurred.

[298] The target must also inform the public with respect to the reaching, exceeding or decreasing below the applicable thresholds within three business days of receiving the relevant notification to that end.

12.13 Exclusivity and Break Fees

[299] The possibility of the target to grant exclusivity to an offeror and/or agree on a break fee is not regulated under Romanian law.

[300] However, as all investors must be treated equally, exclusivity arrangements are not compliant with this principle. Further, regardless of any exclusivity arrangement, a counter-takeover offer may always be initiated.

[301] In addition, the enforcement of break fees is uncertain under Romanian law.

12.14 Due Diligence

[302] Allowing a due diligence review in a listed company raises concerns about breaking market abuse rules. Most of the relevant market abuse rules are concerned with the use or disclosure of privileged information.

[303] The law dictates that privileged information is specific information which has not been made public, which directly or indirectly concerns issuers or financial instruments and which, if made public, could have a significant impact on the price of those financial instruments or on the price of the various ancillary financial instruments. Privileged information is information that is not public and which may be used by an investor to substantiate its investment decision. As any listed company has to comply with significant disclosure requirements and, more specifically, should disclose price-sensitive information, most of such information should have been made public in one form or another over time.

[304] The main concern in setting up a data room is making an appropriate judgment as to how much-privileged information may be disclosed to potential investors in that manner.

[305] In any event, price-sensitive information which has not yet been disclosed should not be provided to potential investors before it becomes public. To this end, we have serious reservations about 'shadow audits' performed by investors at the same time as the auditors, as this would obviously give access to price-sensitive information before such information becomes public. The audited financial statements will, after all, be made public in a relatively short time, and the public, including the investors, will at such time have access to the information set out therein.

[306] It is forbidden to use privileged information for the purposes of sale or acquisition or in connection with an intention to sell or acquire the financial instruments to which such privileged information relates. It is furthermore forbidden to disclose privileged information to any other person, except when the disclosure was made in the normal exercise of an activity or of one's duties as an employee.

[307] Intentionally breaking these interdictions is a criminal offence, punishable with imprisonment. If damage were to be caused to the target or its shareholders by the improper use or disclosure of privileged information, the civil liability (i.e., obligation to pay damages) of the perpetrator would also be engaged. Allowing potential investors to have access to information in relation to the target as part of a due diligence investigation also exposes the relevant person(s) to this liability.

[308] A series of steps are used in practice to reduce such exposure:

(1) executing a confidentiality agreement with the potential investors;
(2) inserting in the agreement with the potential investors an undertaking on their part that they will not purchase or sell any shares in the target before launching the public offer;

(3) ensuring that the due diligence process is transparent and that, in the event that there is more than one potential investor, the same information is provided to all such investors on a non-discriminatory basis; and
(4) publishing all privileged information made available in the data room before any kind of trade on the market (including the launch of a public offer) is effected by the potential investors; this could be done in a variety of ways, including issuing current reports to the Romanian FSA or publishing an annual report (approved in advance by the general meeting of shareholders which would also discharge the directors of the target from liability).

[309] Notwithstanding the above, allowing access to privileged information before making such information public is not risk-free. Shareholders and directors of the target remain exposed to falling foul of the market abuse rules, which restrict them from disclosing privileged information. Given that the object of a due diligence exercise is to acquire information and to use that information to substantiate an investment decision, an investor could fall foul of the market abuse rules, which restrict the use of privileged information in relation to the *intention* to acquire the financial instruments to which such privileged information relate.

[310] For the majority shareholders to be allowed to sell their shares in the target without perpetrating market abuse, they must make sure that all price-sensitive or privileged information referring to the target and its shares is disclosed beforehand. The best approach would constitute a combination of current and periodical reports and the option of a secondary public sale offer, which would entail the publication of a prospectus approved by the Romanian FSA.

[311] A large part of the information to be examined in a normal due diligence exercise is accessible to the public in the form of various public registries or even information published in official publications. This sometimes includes what is normally classified as privileged information or other price-sensitive information: details related to the share capital of the target, the resolutions of its general meetings, details regarding mergers, changes in the direct control of the issuer, changes of directors and managers, changes in the characteristics or rights attached to securities, bankruptcy, permits which are listed in public registers, details regarding immovable properties, securities over movable assets, some details about litigation of lesser importance such as the name of the parties or the nature of the dispute, registered IPR and the audited financial statements of the company.

[312] While the above-mentioned information is not readily accessible to any interested party and involves significant effort in gathering and sorting it out, because it is of a public nature, it cannot be considered privileged information. Thus, disclosing it to a potential investor may expose the issuer to questioning from the Romanian FSA or even a fine over the lack of equality of treatment between investors, but it should not give rise to market abuse charges.

12.15 Announcements

[313] A potential offer must be kept secret until the official announcement of the offer is published.

[314] The offeror may approach the target and lead negotiations with it even prior to the public disclosure of its intention to launch a takeover offer. In such a case, the target is required to protect inside information and prevent any disclosure of the information about the offer unless the information is disclosed on even terms in accordance with the applicable reporting obligations related to the privileged information.

12.16 Minimum Price Obligations

[315] The method for calculating the minimum price is expressly regulated for each type of public offer.

[316] The minimum price in a straightforward public purchase offer is fixed in RON and is the higher of:

(1) the highest price paid by the offeror or by persons acting in concert with offeror within a period of twelve months prior to lodging the bidding documentation with the Romanian FSA; and
(2) the weighted average trading price calculated on the last twelve months prior to lodging the bidding documentation with the Romanian FSA.

[317] In cases where none of the above-mentioned criteria is applicable, the purchase price should be at least equal to the value of the target's net assets per share according to the latest financial statements.

[318] The price to be used with respect to a voluntary takeover is the highest of the following:

(1) the highest price paid by the offeror or by persons acting in concert with the offeror, as the case may be, for shares in the target within the twelve-month period prior to the date of submission to the Romanian FSA of the voluntary takeover documentation;
(2) the weighted average trading price of the shares of the target calculated with respect to the twelve-month period prior to the date of submission with the Romanian FSA of the voluntary takeover documentation; and
(3) the value of the target's net assets per share, taking into account the latest financial statements of the target.

[319] In a mandatory takeover, the price must be the highest price paid by the offeror or by persons acting in concert with the offeror, as the case may be, for shares in the target within the twelve-month period prior to the date of submission to the

Romanian FSA of the mandatory takeover documentation. If the criteria are not applicable, further rules are dictated by the law in establishing the minimum offer price to this end.

[320] The Romanian FSA, as part of its supervisory powers, is required to assess the fairness of the fixed offer price.

12.17 Securities as Consideration

[321] The consideration offered by an offeror may also take the form of securities or a combination of securities and cash.

12.18 Same Terms for All Shareholders

[322] The same terms have to be offered to all shareholders.

[323] All takeover offers must target all the shares in the target not held by the offeror, irrespective of the class of such shares.

[324] No express legal provisions make reference to dealing with options over or convertible securities of the target which existed prior to the commencement of the takeover. Consequently, it may be considered that the ongoing takeover offer does not impact such rights.

12.19 Conditions for a Bid

[325] Certain conditions may be included within the terms of a straightforward public purchase offer (e.g., maximum targeted shareholding). Should the offeror want to include other conditions within the takeover documentation, such conditions must be compliant with the principle of according equal treatment to all shareholders of the target and are subject to the scrutiny of the Romanian FSA.

[326] In addition, given the irrevocable nature of a takeover, such takeover may not be conditional, for example, on a minimum quota or subscription rate in order to close the takeover.

12.20 Timetable

[327] The timeline of a public offer is outlined in the table below (this table covers all the steps of a voluntary takeover; the preliminary announcement and the target's board of directors considered position are two steps which do not apply in the context of a straightforward public purchase offer):

No.	*Timing*	*Action*
1.	D-day	Submission of the preliminary announcement with the Romanian FSA
2.	+ 30 calendar days	Approval by the Romanian FSA of the preliminary announcement
3.	+ 5 business days	(i) Sending the preliminary announcement to the target company and to the BSE and (ii) publishing the preliminary announcement in national and local daily newspapers
4.	+ 5 business days (from receipt of the preliminary announcement by the target company)	Target company's board of directors sending to the Romanian FSA, the BSE and the purchaser its considered position with respect to the voluntary public offer
5.	+ 30 calendar days (from publishing of the preliminary announcement)	Submitting the request for the approval of the offer prospectus with the Romanian FSA
6.	+ 10 business days	Romanian FSA authorization decision with respect to the offer prospectus
7.	+ 2 business days	Publishing of the offer announcement and offer prospectus + Offer prospectus lodged with the BSE
8.	+ 3 business days (from publishing of the offer announcement)	Launch of the offer
9.	+ 10 business days through 50 business days	Minimum and maximum offer period (as provided under the approved offer prospectus)
10.	+ 1 business day	Transaction day (T)
11.	+ 3 business day	Settlement of the transaction (T+3)
12.	+ 3 business days	Maximum period for offer price payment

No.	*Timing*	*Action*
13.	+ 5 business days from offer closing (from the date of the elapsing of the offer period – as per item 9 of this table)	Maximum period for submission to the Romanian FSA and the BSE of the report on the outcome of the offer + Making public the report on the outcome of the offer on the website of the BSE
14.	+ 10 business days from submission of the report on the outcome of the offer	Confirmation from the Romanian FSA with respect to the receipt of the report on the outcome of the offer

12.21 Counteroffers

[328] Any person who wishes to launch a counteroffer must do so by filing the proper documentation with the Romanian FSA within ten business days from the date the takeover offer has been made public. The price offered in such a counteroffer must exceed by at least 5% the price in the initial offer and must have as object at least the same number of shares or must target at least the same participation in the share capital.

[329] In its decision on whether to authorize such a counteroffer, the Romanian FSA must also decide the date by which all competing offers must be closed, as well as a final date for submitting for approval any increases in the offer price. Once the date has been set for the submission of any increases in the offer price, based on specific procedural rules, an auction for the adjudication of the highest price will take place at the Romanian FSA's headquarters. The date for completion of the offers must not exceed sixty business days from the start of the first offer.

12.22 Content of Documents

[330] The offer documents are regulated materials and are subject to the prior approval of the Romanian FSA.

[331] The outline of the relevant documents below is applicable to straightforward public purchase offers and voluntary takeovers (except for the preliminary announcement, which is relevant in the context of the voluntary takeover approval process only).

[332] When the decision to make a voluntary public offer has been taken by the offeror, it must submit for approval, without undue delay, to the Romanian FSA a draft preliminary announcement and certain documents required by law.

[333] Once the draft preliminary announcement is submitted to the Romanian FSA, the offeror, the intermediary and any parties acting in concert with the offeror, as the case may be, may not carry out any transactions in relation to the securities in the target until the opening of the voluntary public offer.

12.22.1 Content of the Preliminary Announcement

[334] The minimum content of the preliminary announcement is as follows:

(a) the identification details of the target (including business name, registered office, fiscal code);
(b) the identification details of the offeror (including business name, registered office, value of the subscribed and paid share capital and the structure of the shareholding);
(c) the number of shares in the target held by the offeror and by the group of persons acting in concert with the offeror;
(d) the number of securities subject to the voluntary public offer;
(e) the minimum offered price – to be submitted in a sealed envelope; this section in the preliminary announcement will need to be left blank upon submission to the Romanian FSA and will be filled in after approval of the preliminary announcement;
(f) the name of the intermediary;
(g) the objectives of the offeror in relation to the target, in particular with respect to any personnel and management changes within the target and the strategic development plans of both the target and the offeror which will have an impact on the employment policies of the offeror and on the locations where the activities of both companies are carried out; and
(h) financial and economic data of the offeror pursuant to the latest financial reports (including total assets, total own capital, turnover and financial results).

12.22.2 Documents Accompanying the Preliminary Announcement

[335] The following documents must be attached to the preliminary announcement (in the context of a straightforward public purchase offer, the offer documentation consists only of the documents referred to below, and the preliminary announcement is not part of the approval process):

(a) draft offer prospectus;
(b) draft offer announcement;
(c) a notarized statement by the offeror regarding the price offered within the voluntary public offer – to be submitted in a sealed envelope;

(d) either (a) evidence of a bank deposit equal to at least 30% of the total value of the offer which is being made (the account must be in the name of the intermediary, and this amount must be blocked for the period in which the offer is open) or (b) a bank letter of guarantee equal to 100% of the value of the offer, issued in favour of the intermediary and valid until the settlement of the transaction;
(e) a copy of the intermediary agreement concluded between the offeror and the intermediary;
(f) a notarized statement by the offeror as to the persons with whom the offeror is acting in concert with respect to the target, as the case may be;
(g) a notarized statement by the offeror and the legal documentation showing the price at which the offeror and the persons acting in concert with the offeror, as the case may be, have acquired shares in the target;
(h) a notarized statement by the offeror that all documents submitted to the Romanian FSA are true copies of the originals thereof and reflect the current characteristics of the offeror;
(i) a notarized statement by the intermediary concerning any potential conflicts of interest with the offeror and/or other clients;
(j) evidence of the registration of the offeror and the persons with whom it acts in concert with the relevant public authority in their incorporation/home state;
(k) the constitutive/founding documents of the offeror and of the persons with whom it acts in concert and any amendments thereof, together with evidence of registration of such documents with the relevant public authorities;
(l) legal documents evidencing the shareholding structure of the offeror up to the ultimate beneficial owner (for listed companies up to the shareholders holding at least 1% of the share capital); and
(m) the synthetic structure of the shareholding of the target and securities account statements of the purchaser and any person acting in concert indicating their holding in the target, as the case may be;
(n) the report prepared by an independent valuator, authorized and registered with the Romanian FSA;
(o) draft of engagement of the intermediaries regarding their compliance with the offer conditions; and
(p) other information or documents considered to be necessary by the Romanian FSA.

12.22.3 Content of the Offer Prospectus

[336] The offer prospectus must contain the following information:

(a) identification and other various details in relation to the target and the offeror (including registered office, fiscal code, value of share capital and structure of the shareholding of each);
(b) financial and economic information of the offeror in accordance with the latest approved financial statements (total assets, total own capital, turnover, financial results);

(c) identification details of any persons acting in concert with the offeror or with the target (including the type of company, business name, registered office, relationship with purchaser or target, as the case may be);
(d) the number of shares in the target held by the offeror and by all the persons with whom it acts in concert;
(e) the number and class of the shares subject to the voluntary public offer;
(f) the offer price and calculation of such price*; this section in the offer prospectus will need to be left blank upon submission to the Romanian FSA and will be filled in after approval of the preliminary announcement*;
(g) date of launch of the offer, date of expiry of the offer and details of any option for an extension;
(h) with respect to subscription/acceptance of the offer: the location, the method and the time;
(i) the source and the amount of funds used to carry out the proposed transaction, including the terms of any loans or other financing sources;
(j) all the conditions that the offer must comply with;
(k) the offeror's plans regarding the change of management, liquidation of the target, change in the business activity or de-listing from a regulated market;
(l) the position of the board of directors and/or of the general extraordinary meeting of shareholders of the target with respect to the opportunity of the voluntary offer – *this section in the offer prospectus will need to be left blank upon submission to the Romanian FSA; but will be filled in after receipt of such position and submitted to the Romanian FSA together with the request for the approval of the offer prospectus*; and
(m) the national legislation which will apply to the agreements concluded between the offeror and the persons holding shares in the target as a result of the offer, as well as the competent courts of law;
(n) any other information considered relevant by the offeror;
(o) any other information which may be deemed necessary by the Romanian FSA for the purpose of protecting the investors.

[337] The information included in the offer prospectus must be certified, among others, by the purchaser and by the intermediary, each of them being held liable, as the case may be and depending on the person drafting the offer prospectus, for its truthfulness, correctness and completeness.

12.22.4 Content of the Offer Announcement

[338] The offer announcement must contain basic information in relation to the offeror and the target securities for which the offer is being made, as follows:

(a) the name and the registered office of the target;
(b) the name and the registered office of the offeror;
(c) the number of shares subject to the offer;
(d) the offer price – to be submitted in a sealed envelope; this section in the offer announcement will need to be left blank upon submission to the Romanian FSA but will be filled in after approval of the preliminary announcement;

(e) the name of the intermediary;
(f) the number of shares in the target held by the offeror and its concert parties;
(g) the statement that an offer prospectus has been drafted and further details on where the offer prospectus has been made available;
(h) the place and time schedule during which the hard copy version of the offer prospectus is made available; and
(i) the period for which the offer is open – this section is left blank; upon submission, we only indicate the offer period in business days; relevant dates will be filled in after the approval.

12.23 Rules about Advertising

[339] No advertising can be made in relation to a takeover offer without the prior approval of the Romanian FSA. The advertising materials must be lodged with the Romanian FSA at least seven business days prior to the offer closing and must be made available to the public as of the date the offer prospectus is published and until one business day prior to the offer closing at the latest.

[340] All information provided in advertising materials must be correct, complete, precise and in accordance with the content of the takeover documentation and must make reference to the place where and the date on which the takeover documentation is available. In addition, any information provided verbally or in writing (including in electronic format) regarding the takeover offer, even if without an advertising character, must be in accordance with the information provided in the takeover documentation.

12.24 Withdrawal of Offers

[341] The public offer is launched after the elapse of a period of three business days from the date on which the offer announcement has been made public. The launch date and the offer expiry date to this end are indicated in the offer announcement and in the offer prospectus based on the Romanian FSA's decision on approval. The offer cannot be withdrawn from the date it has been launched as indicated above.

12.25 Passing of Control

[342] The transfer of ownership rights over the securities acquired within the public offer takes place upon the settlement of the transaction on the exchange market. The transaction in relation to the offer is settled after the offer closes on a specific section to this end of the market (T+3). Payment by the offeror in respect of the subscribing shareholders needs to be made within not more than three business days from the date of settlement of the transaction.

12.26 Compulsory Purchase Procedures

[343] Following a public offer addressed to all shareholders and for the entire stakes they hold in the target, the offeror has the right to require the shareholders who did not accept the offer to sell their stakes to the offeror at a fair price, provided that one of the following conditions is met:

(1) the offeror holds shares representing 95% of the aggregate number of shares with voting rights in the target's share capital and at least 95% of the voting rights that may be effectively exercised; or
(2) the offeror has acquired, under the offer, shares representing at least 90% of the aggregate number of shares with voting rights in the target's share capital shares with voting rights and at least 90% of the voting rights targeted under the offer (namely, at least 90% of the voting rights which were the subject of the public offer).

[344] The offeror may exercise its right to squeeze out the minority shareholders within three months from the date the public offer has been closed.

[345] Conversely, a minority shareholder may, following a public offer addressed to all shareholders and for the entire stake they hold in the target, request the offeror that holds shares pursuant to any of the scenarios above to purchase the shares of the minority shareholder at a fair price.

[346] Should the target have more than one class of shares, the rules are applicable to each class of shares separately.

[347] The price and the procedural steps for the squeeze out/buy out are subject to strictly regulated procedures and timetables.

12.27 Enforcement of Rules on Public Takeovers

[348] Breach of the relevant takeover rules constitutes an administrative offence. Such administrative offences are enforced by the Romanian FSA. The sanctions imposed may range from warnings to fines as high as a percentage of the annual turnover of the perpetrator.

[349] Further sanctions that may be imposed include the following:

(1) suspending the exercise of the voting rights;
(2) suspending the shares from trading;
(3) invalidating the offer; or
(4) invalidating the share acquisitions.

[350] Also, if intentional, a breach of certain takeover rules (e.g., insider trading) could also result in a criminal offence sanctioned with fines or imprisonment.

[351] In certain situations, the civil liability (i.e., obligation to pay damages) of the perpetrator would also be engaged.

12.28 Other Relevant Laws and Due Diligence Issues

[352] In Romania, criminal offences of bribery and corruption (e.g., receiving bribes, giving bribes, influencing trafficking, influencing buying and failure to report a criminal offence of corruption) are mainly provided under the Romanian Criminal Code, Law no. 78/2000 regarding the prevention, discovery and sanctioning of acts of corruption and under Law no. 129/2019 for preventing and fighting money laundering and terrorist financing, as well as for amending and supplementing certain legislative acts.

[353] With respect to the enforcement of anti-corruption/anti-bribery laws in Romania, the specific prosecution authority in this respect in Romania is the National Anti-Corruption Directorate (the '*DNA*').

[354] According to the DNA annual report for 2022 (the '*DNA Report*'), the DNA has completed 2 087 criminal pursuits and provided indictments in 404 cases (which relate to 779 persons, of which 52 were legal persons). This constitutes an increase from 2021 when the DNA provided indictments in 338 cases (which relate to 730 persons, of which 51 were legal persons).

[355] The 2 087 completed criminal pursuits have been finalized as follows: (i) 816 after more than one year from the date the initial complaint was filed; and (ii) 519 after more than two years from the date the initial complaint was filed.

[356] With respect to final decisions issued by the courts, the DNA Report mentions that, in 2022, 287 final decisions were issued with respect to 439 persons having been indicted by the DNA. In addition, in 2022, the courts issued decisions (which are not yet final) in 105 cases and with respect to 226 persons.

[357] According to the DNA Report, the DNA has cooperated with similar entities in other countries, including with relevant entities in the United Kingdom and in the US.

[358] The corruption perception index calculated by Transparency International yearly indicates that Romania's score has increased from 38 of 100 in 2008 to 46 of 100 in 2022. This score ranks Romania in 63rd place in 2022 of 180 places.

12.29 Money Laundering Regulations

[359] Law no. 129/2019 for preventing and fighting money laundering and terrorist financing, as well as for amending and supplementing certain legislative acts (the '*Anti-Money Laundering Law*') and related secondary legislation, including the main Romanian legal provisions regarding money laundering and terrorist financing.

[360] The public entity having regulatory, surveillance and control powers in this respect is the National Office for Prevention and Control of Money Laundering and, if applicable, by case, the National Bank of Romania, the Romanian FSA and the Romanian National Gambling Office. In addition, it also receives, analyses and processes reports of suspicious acts related to money.

[361] The main money laundering offences under the Anti-Money Laundering Law are as follows:

(a) the exchange or transfer of goods, knowing that the goods derive from the perpetration of a criminal offence, with the following purpose:
   - hiding or disguising the illegal source of the goods; or
   - aiding the person who perpetrated the criminal offence to avoid prosecution, criminal proceedings before a court or the imposition of a criminal sanction.

(b) hiding or disguising the true nature of the origin, location, placement, circulation or ownership of the goods or the rights over the goods, knowing that the goods originated from a criminal offence; or

(c) acquiring, retaining or using assets by a person other than the offender, knowing that the assets originated from a criminal offence.

[362] In addition, the main administrative offences provided under the Anti-Money Laundering Law are as follows:

- the use by the reporting entity's employees of the confidential information received due to the Anti-Money Laundering Law requirements for personnel interest;
- disclosure by the reporting entities, their management, managers and employees of the information held in connection with actions of money laundering and terrorism financing to their clients that are subject to such offences;
- failure to comply with the obligation to report to the National Office for Prevention and Control of Money Laundering the suspicions of money laundering; and
- failure to adopt and implement adequate 'know your customer' measures in certain situations.

12.30 Environmental and Product Safety Laws

[363] The main regulatory act in the environmental field is the Government Emergency Ordinance no. 195/2005 on environmental protection, which sets out the general principles and obligations related to environmental protection.

[364] Different other regulatory acts may be applicable in the environmental field, depending on the project developed and operated. In this respect, the below regulatory acts have to be taken into consideration and followed by the economic operators who carry out activities which impact or may have an impact on the environment:

(1) Law no. 278/2013 on industrial emissions, which aims to ensure the prevention and control of pollution, establishing rules designed to prevent (or, where that is not practicable, to reduce) emissions into air, water and land and to prevent the generation of waste, in order to achieve a high level of protection of the environment taken as a whole. Also, this law establishes the conditions and procedures to follow in order to obtain integrated environmental authorization. This regulatory act transposes into the Romanian legislation Directive no. 2010/75/EU.
(2) Law no. 107/1996 on waters providing rules on water resources protection and establishing different obligations for economic operators who carry out activities on waters or in relation to waters.
(3) Government Emergency Ordinance no. 92/2021 on waste regime repealing Law no. 211/2011 on waste regime. This enactment has been adopted in order to ensure full transposition into the Romanian legislation of Directive no. 2018/851. New obligations on waste management may be applicable to the waste producers, including specific obligations regarding the extended producer liability.
(4) Government Decision 1074/2021 on the guarantee-return system for primary non-returnable packaging establishing the responsibilities for the collection, transport and recycling of primary non-returnable packaging. According to the provisions of this enactment, consumers will pay a deposit when buying a bottled drink, and after emptying the packaging, they will have to return it to receive the amount of the deposit paid initially.
(5) Government Ordinance no. 6/2021 on the reduction of certain plastic products on the environment, having the main purpose of reducing the single-use plastic products from different industries. According to the provisions of this enactment, economic operators have the obligation to progressively reduce the quantities of certain plastic products placed on the market starting with 2023 (e.g., beverage glasses, including their lids or food containers). Moreover, other certain single-use plastic products are forbidden to be placed on the market from the date when the new enactment enters into force. Certain single-use plastic products are ear drumsticks or plastic straws, except those used in medical activities.
(6) Government Ordinance no. 2/2021 on the landfill of waste repealing Government Decision no. 349/2005 on the landfill of waste. The main purpose of this enactment is to regulate and classify landfills, provide authorization criteria, acceptance of waste in landfills, and closure of certain landfills.
(7) Government Emergency Ordinance no. 68/2007 regarding the environmental liability with respect to the prevention and remedying of environmental damage, which transposed into Romanian legislation Directive no. 2004/35/EC. The main purpose of this enactment is to ensure a unitary and separate legal framework as regards environmental damages and also to establish the legal framework for environmental liability based on the '*polluter's pay principle* in order to prevent and remedy environmental damages.

(8) Government Emergency Ordinance no. 196/2005 on Environmental Fund establishes the main attributions of the Environmental Fund Administration and the main payment obligations of the producers who place on the market different products which generate waste.
(9) Government Emergency Ordinance no. 57/2007 regarding the regime of protected natural areas, preservation of natural habitats, of wild flora and fauna. The main purpose of this enactment is to ensure the conservation and sustainable use of the natural heritage, which is considered a major public interest objective.
(10) Government Emergency Ordinance no. 43/2007 on integration in the environment of genetically modified organisms. The main purpose of this enactment is to ensure the legislative and institutional framework for carrying out activities with genetically modified organisms, considering the caution principle in order to ensure the protection of human health and the environment.
(11) Law no. 104/2011 regarding the ambient air quality, which transposed into Romanian legislation Directive no. 2008/50/CE. The main purpose of this enactment is to establish different national measures and obligations for public authorities and economic operators as regards the quality of the ambient air.
(12) Government Decision no. 1076/2004 regarding the procedure for environmental assessment of plans and programmes. This regulatory act establishes the environmental assessment procedure ('SEA procedure') for certain plans and programmes which may have an impact on the environment.
(13) Law no. 292/2018 on the impact assessment of certain public and private projects on the environment, which transposed into Romanian legislation Directive no. 2011/92/EU. This regulatory act establishes the impact of environmental assessment procedure ('EIA procedure') for certain projects which may have an impact on the environment.
(14) Law no. 249/2015 on packaging and waste packaging mainly regulates different obligations for the producers who place packaging on the market. These obligations are established in order to ensure proper management of the packaging placed on the market and of the waste packaging generated so as to prevent and reduce environmental impact.
(15) Law no. 74/2019 on the management of potentially contaminated and contaminated sites. The main purpose of this regulatory act is to establish different obligations for public authorities and economic operators in order to identify and ensure remedy for the contaminated sites.
(16) Law No. 246/2020 on using, conservation and protection of the soil, which mainly regulates the activities related to the use, conservation, improvement, assessment of the bioproductive capacity, economic improvement, soil protection and integrated monitoring of the soil quality.
(17) Order no. 1798/2007 on approving the procedure for issuance of the environmental authorizations. This regulatory act establishes the activities which require and have to obtain environmental authorization. Also, this

regulatory act provides the main steps which have to be followed by an economic operator in order to require and obtain the environmental permit.

(18) Order no. 1150/2020 on approving the procedure regarding the granting of annual visas for environmental permits and integrated environmental permits. This regulatory act establishes the main obligation for the economic operators who hold an environmental/integrated environmental authorization to apply for the annual visa so that these regulatory acts to maintain their validity.

(19) Law no. 111/1996 regarding the security deployment, regulation, authorization and control of nuclear activities. The main purpose of this enactment is related to the authorization and control of nuclear activities carried out for exclusively peaceful purposes in accordance with the regulations and obligations arising from international conventions.

[365] *Product liability* is mainly regulated by:

(1) Government Ordinance no. 21/1992 regarding consumer protection, as republished and further supplemented and amended.
(2) Government Emergency Ordinance no. 140/2021 on certain aspects of contracts for the sale of goods, as further amended.
(3) Law no. 245/2004 regarding the general safety of products, as republished.
(4) Law no. 240/2004 regarding liability for defective products, as republished and further supplemented and amended.

[366] Under this legislation, manufacturers, importers and, under certain circumstances, distributors and sellers are liable for defective products or products that do not comply with the sale and purchase agreement. Any contractual clause excluding or limiting consumers' legal rights is null and void unless otherwise provided by the law. Special rules apply to certain categories of products.

12.31 Intellectual Property Rights

[367] At a national level, there are certain types of IPR that may be registered with the relevant entity, the State Office for Patents and Trademarks ('*OSIM*') or the Romanian Copyright Office ('*ORDA*'). Set out below is a brief description of the registration, protection and enforcement possibilities under Romanian law concerning the main classes of IPR.

12.31.1 Registration of IPR

[368] Registration requests concerning certain IPR at a national level must include certain documentation, as provided for under the relevant law. Further enquiries or documentation may be requested by the relevant registration entity, if applicable.

[369] A patent may be registered with OSIM regarding an invention in a technological field provided that the relevant invention: (i) is new; (ii) involves an inventive activity; and (iii) is susceptible to industrial application.

[370] A trademark may be registered with OSIM provided that it is:

(i) any sign (e.g., words, including personal names or designs, letters, numerals, colours, figurative elements) (a) capable of distinguishing the goods or services of one undertaking from those of other undertakings; and which (b) is represented in the Trademarks Register in such a way as to enable the competent authorities and the public to establish clearly and precisely the subject matter of the protection conferred to the owner;
(ii) distinctive;
(iii) available (i.e., not affected by prior IPR); and
(iv) lawful.

[371] Designs and models may be registered with OSIM provided that: (i) they are new; and (ii) they have an individual character.

[372] Utility models may be registered with OSIM provided that they: (i) represent technical inventions (greater than a simple professional handiness); (ii) are new; and (iii) are susceptible to industrial application.

[373] The protection of computer programs includes the protection of any expression of a computer program, application programs, operating systems (expressed in any language – either source code or object code), preparatory conceptual material and relevant manuals. Computer programs may be registered with ORDA. However, the existence of IPR related to computer programs is not subject to the registration thereof.

[374] IPR related to databases are recognized as copyright IPR under Romanian law, and the existence of IPR related to databases is not subject to the registration thereof.

12.31.2 Protection and Enforcement of IPR

[375] The protection period varies depending on the type of IPR: (a) registered patents – twenty years from the filing of a complete application; (b) registered trademarks – ten years from the filing date, renewable for subsequent ten-year periods; (c) designs and models – a maximum of twenty-five years, including renewals; (d) utility models – a maximum of ten years, including renewals; (e) copyright and computer programs – as a matter of principle, patrimonial rights regarding copyright are protected during their author's (natural person's) lifetime and the seventy years following his/her death, while the non-patrimonial rights are transmissible by way of succession for an unlimited period of time; and (f) databases – fifteen years from 1 January of the year subsequent to the year of completion of the database.

[376] The holders of IPR or other interested persons may opt for civil, administrative and criminal claims with respect to IPR. Assurance measures may be taken by a

court (e.g., prohibiting the continuance of the infringement of the IPR, setting in place a guarantee for future damages to be awarded to the IPR holder) in accordance with the relevant legislation. Further, damages may be awarded by a court for the infringement of IPR in accordance with the relevant legislation.

[377] Set out below is a brief summary of the main additional claims that may be brought.

12.31.3 Patents

[378] Any person, under certain circumstances, may request the revocation of a patent within six months from the publication of its award (e.g., it does not fulfil the patentability conditions). A response to the revocation request must be given within three months of its filing with the relevant OSIM department.

[379] Further, an annulment request may be filed by a person with the relevant court (except in circumstances where a revocation request must be filed) regarding a patent under certain circumstances (e.g., it does not fulfil the patentability conditions, the holder of the patent is not the person entitled to hold it).

[380] Further, criminal claims may be filed, among other things, if a person claims to be an inventor of a patented invention without having any rights in this respect or for counterfeiting a patented invention.

12.31.4 Trademarks

[381] Any interested person may, under certain circumstances (e.g., where a mark is identical to a registered trademark and it addresses the same type of services), file an opposition against the registration of a trademark within two months of the date when the admittance of the trademark registration is published after the absolute grounds of refusal are checked by OSIM. In this case, OSIM notifies the trademark applicant about the lodged opposition, allowing the parties a cooling-off period of two months for an amicable settlement. Upon the mutual request of the parties, such period may be extended with an additional term, which cannot exceed three months.

[382] Any interested person may request annulment of a registered trademark at any time during its period of protection to the extent that the conditions for its valid registration were not observed. Also, a civil action may be brought in court for the counterfeit of a registered trademark or administrative proceedings may be initiated before OSIM.

[383] Further, criminal claims may be filed, among other matters, for the counterfeit of a registered trademark.

12.31.5 Designs and Models

[384] Any interested person may, under certain circumstances (e.g., where the person requesting the registration is not entitled to register the IPR, or the design or model incorporates a work protected by copyright or another IPR), file an opposition against the registration of a design or model within two months from the publication of the request for registration thereof.

[385] Furthermore, criminal claims may be filed, *inter alia*, for the counterfeit of a registered design or model.

12.31.6 Utility Models

[386] The registration of a utility model may be annulled under certain circumstances (e.g., the holder of the utility model was not entitled to obtain it).

12.31.7 Copyright

[387] The relevant legal provisions stipulate a wide variety of criminal offences related to copyright.

[388] Criminal claims that may be filed include, among others, claims for: (i) reproduction of computer programs on IT systems (e.g., by way of installation, storing, running, execution); and (ii) making available to the public databases without any rights in this respect.

12.31.8 Due Diligence

[389] As regards verifications for due diligence purposes, at the national level, both OSIM and ORDA maintain online databases regarding certain registered IPR (e.g., patents, trademarks, designs and models and computer programs), which are searchable for some of the registered IPR in respect of certain criteria (e.g., holder of the IPR, name or registration number of the IPR). In addition, there is an accessible online database concerning*.ro* domain names evidencing the holder of a specific domain name.

12.32 Agents and Distributors

[390] As provided by the Civil Code, through an agency agreement, the principal empowers the agent, on a continuing basis, either (i) to negotiate (only) or (ii) to negotiate and to conclude agreements in the name and on behalf of the principal, in exchange for remuneration, the power/authority of the agent being limited to one or more specific geographical regions.

[391] The agent is considered an independent intermediary who acts as a professional and is entitled to remuneration for all the agreements concluded as a result of its intermediation.

[392] Whatever the terms of the mandate agreement or the commission agreement, the agent is entitled to remuneration for an agreement concluded even after the termination of the agency agreement, provided that the following conditions are met:

(1) the agreement was concluded mainly due to the involvement of the agent during the agency agreement, and the conclusion took place within a reasonable period of time from the termination thereof; and
(2) the order issued by the third party was received by the principal or by the agent prior to the termination of the agency agreement.

12.32.1 Termination Remuneration for the Agent

[393] Upon termination of the agency agreement, the agent is entitled to receive from the principal a specific remuneration for termination, provided that the following conditions are cumulatively met:

(1) the agent has procured new clients to the principal or has significantly increased the volume of the principal's transactions with existing clients, and the principal is still substantially benefiting from these activities of the agent; and
(2) the payment of such remuneration is fair, taking into account the value of the agent's remuneration in respect of the above transactions as well as the possible diminution of the agent's professional activity due to a possible non-competition clause.

[394] The value of the remuneration cannot exceed the value of the annual remuneration, computed as the average annual value for the previous five years or for the entire duration of the agency agreement if the contractual period is less than five years.

[395] Exceptionally, the agent shall not be entitled to such termination remuneration if:

(1) the principal terminates the agency agreement due to the agent's breach of obligations;
(2) the agent unilaterally terminates the agreement, except for cases where such termination is due to age, infirmity or disease of the agent, in view of which it cannot reasonably be required to continue its activity;
(3) assignment of the agency agreement by replacing the agent with a third party; or
(4) unless otherwise agreed by the parties, in cases of novation, whereby the agent is replaced with a third party.

[396] Distribution agreements are not regulated by the Civil Code. Therefore, any mandatory compensation or other indemnities on termination could be triggered only if the parties agreed to this in the relevant agreement.

12.33 Valuation of Intangible Assets

[397] Intellectual capital is recognized as the most important asset of many of the world's largest and most powerful companies. It is often the key objective in mergers and acquisitions, and knowledgeable companies are increasingly using licensing routes to transfer these assets to low tax jurisdictions.

[398] In order to establish the value of these assets according to International Valuation Standards (the 'IVS'), the notion of market value is used. Market value is the estimated amount for which an asset or liability should be exchanged on the valuation date between a willing buyer and a willing seller in an arm's length transaction after proper marketing and where the parties had each acted knowledgeably, prudently and without compulsion (IVS, 2022). This is the most frequent type of value that is resorted to in the process of evaluation.

[399] Financial reports use the notion of fair value. Fair value is the price that would be received to sell an asset or paid to transfer a liability in an orderly transaction between market participants at the measurement date.

[400] The appraisal of intangible assets sometimes involves particular appraisal aspects which have been determined mainly by the particular characteristic features of these assets.

[401] One of the aspects which could trigger difficulties within the valuation process of intellectual capital is the method of its acquisition. Intangible assets that have been purchased separately are evaluated at their acquisition cost. The acquisition cost includes the purchase price to which the following may be added: direct expenses that can be attributed to the relevant asset, expenses for the registration of the asset (patents, brands, etc.), testing expenses, non-refundable fees, etc. Intangible assets internally generated are evaluated at production cost, which includes expenses for used materials and services, salaries and other staff expenses, directly attributable expenses (fees, patent and licence amortization) and a share of indirect expenses.

[402] Intangible assets purchased in exchange for other assets and those purchased as part of a larger business combination are evaluated at their fair value on the purchase date. The initial setting of an intangible element against current expenses prevents the latter from being recognized subsequently as part of the cost of an intangible asset. In fact, subsequent expenses will increase the value of an intangible asset only if they are going to generate future benefits that go beyond the initial performance level and can be evaluated in a credible way.

12.34 'Change of Control' Clauses

[403] 'Change of control' clauses are commonly used in loan agreements, and they are generally enforceable. They cover both the obligation to notify and, in most cases, the obligation to obtain the consent of the other party to share transfers or other similar corporate changes.

[404] We would expect to find such clauses, particularly in banking loan arrangements of the target company, especially in the loan agreements concluded after 2008 (the onset of the global financial crisis). 'Change of control' clauses stipulated in loan agreements usually enable banks to declare an event of default or a mandatory prepayment event and thereby cancel any obligation to make further loans and to require the repayment of existing loans.

12.35 The Due Diligence Process

[405] Romania offers attractive opportunities for investment, acquisitions and business partnerships ranging from joint ventures and licensing agreements to distributorships and franchises. However, with this wide range of opportunities come new risks. Generally, potential investors (especially foreign investors) understand that it is advisable to engage reputable legal counsel, both international and Romanian, and to maintain contact with such firms throughout the course of the investment process. However, one cannot say the same for local sellers who do not always engage reputable lawyers in a due diligence process.

[406] Even if, back in the pre-crisis era, comprehensive due diligence was more often performed whenever a transaction was considered in Romania, currently, the number of full due diligence reports has decreased significantly – mostly as a means of cutting costs. It is more and more common to find that not all types of investigations are comprehensively carried out in the context of the due diligence process (e.g., not all fields that could have a connection with the transaction), but only a red flag analysis of those fields likely to have a material impact on the core elements of the business.

[407] As regards investigations regarding immovable properties in Romania, the most common and basic check in this respect is obtaining a Land Book excerpt of the immovable property. Given that a full title check is a very burdensome process which usually does not result in a clear check of the title, it is not a widespread practice to perform a *full* title check of immovable properties located in Romania.

[408] The type of data room used in a due diligence process depends largely on the value/importance of the transaction. Professional investors commonly, if not invariably, request and establish electronic data rooms, while local investors more often undertake only a simple check of the most recent titles/documents (e.g., the latest sale–purchase agreement representing the seller's title).

12.36 Critical Aspects of Due Diligence Investigations

[409] Recently, the most complex legal due diligence operations have been in real estate transactions, banking transactions and privatizations. The 'critical' aspect of each due diligence process mainly depends on: (i) the industry involved in the transaction (e.g., if it is a highly regulated activity in banking transactions); and (ii) the type of the transaction, namely whether it is a share deal or an asset deal.

[410] For example, one of the most complicated parts of a legal due diligence contemplated as an immovable asset deal is the review of information regarding the title to the relevant asset. Apart from the fact that it takes time and skill to identify and collect the relevant documents, which in most cases are not *all* available for review, it is essential to fully comprehend their legal effects, in particular when it comes to the historical transfer of ownership, by spotting any deficiencies that might lead to legal hazards, and finally to advise on the most effective approach towards such findings in negotiating the transaction.

[411] Another aspect that is important to understand in the context of a due diligence process is that Romanian authorities continue to work on slow and bureaucratic procedures. Even though due diligence is substantially based on the analysis of documents provided by the investor's counterpart, information from public sources should not be underestimated. There is a wide range of public sources, such as the Trade Registry, the Land Book, the National Registry for Security Interest, the State Office for Inventions and Trademarks, the BSE and the Credit Bureau, which could provide important information on the target provided the timeline for the due diligence permits undertaking the necessary bureaucratic steps for obtaining such relevant documentation/information.

[412] One of the other important challenges in any due diligence process is the requirement for knowledge of applicable regulations, both primary and secondary Romanian legislation, as well as EU law. Over the last twenty years, Romania's legal framework has evolved into a web of regulatory branches, many of them interlaced and ambiguous, which are undergoing continuous amendment.

12.37 Organization of the Due Diligence Process

[413] As a practical matter, one of the most important requirements for a fruitful due diligence report is a proper 'organization' of the process. This has several meanings for the overall process, for example: (i) a well-organized data room (irrespective of whether the data room is provided in electronic or physical form), especially for international transactions where documents are available for multiple jurisdictions in the same database; and/or (ii) a good management of the due diligence steps upfront (e.g., proper planning to circulate questions and answers between the parties in a consistent manner, to analyse and insert all findings in the final report and/or to allow, from a time perspective, several data exchanges between the parties in this respect).

12.38 Relationship Between the Due Diligence Process and the Contract

[414] The underlying purpose of the due diligence process is to provide the parties to a transaction with the information necessary to draft/prepare the contractual

representations, warranties and indemnities. The extent to which contractual representations, warranties and indemnities are used in Romania depends on several factors, such as: (i) the value of the transaction; or (ii) the sophistication of the parties (professional investors as opposed to local medium or small players). However, the general tendency is to more often make use of these contractual tools, even if the case law on their enforcement/breach has not yet clarified their impact on a transaction.

[415] Under Romanian law, if a party breaches its contractual obligations, the contractual counterparty is entitled to receive damages for its loss if it can prove that either (i) the loss directly resulted from the non-performance of such contractual obligation or (ii) the loss results from a culpable performance of the contractual obligation. Therefore, if a party can prove the existence of a loss resulting from an action/omission of its contractual counterparty, irrespective of whether this involves breach of the contractual representations, warranties and indemnity clauses, the contractual liability of the counterparty can be engaged, provided that all the following conditions are cumulatively met:

(1) one of the parties has incurred a loss;
(2) the counterparty acted in breach of its obligations (on a case-by-case basis, this could be interpreted as breach of the representations, warranties and indemnity provisions);
(3) the counterparty's misconduct is guilt-based (as per the Civil Code, the guilt is presumed in cases of contractual liability therefore the party in breach should prove that its action/omission was triggered by independent causes of fault); and
(4) existence of a cause-action relationship between the counterparty's action/omission and the loss (as provided by the Civil Code, such causality relationship is presumed in cases of contractual liability).

[416] As regards the particular case of a sale and purchase agreement, the seller is under an obligation to provide the buyer with a warranty against hidden defects/flaws. Therefore, if the buyer proves that a breach of the representations, warranties and indemnity provisions resulted in a decrease in the asset's value, the buyer is entitled to seek remedies. The parties may extend, without any limitations, or may minimize, or even exempt (but within certain limitations provided by law) the seller's liability for hidden defects/flaws.

[417] Although it is possible under Romanian law to limit or exclude liability in a contract, such limitations are unenforceable in cases of gross negligence or intentional breach.

[418] If the above conditions of the contractual liability or of the decrease in the asset's value are proved before a court as a result of a breach of the representations, warranties and/or indemnity provisions, the contractual counterparty can:

(1) request termination of the agreement (if the breach/decrease of value is proved to be material for entering into the transaction); and

(2) seek damages (the Civil Code allows the parties to mutually agree on the amount of the damages upfront; otherwise, the level of the damages should also be proved by the counterparty).

12.39 Role of the Courts

[419] The courts represent the main relevant dispute resolution mechanism used in Romania. The courts are not usually biased when it comes to disputes between domestic residents and foreigners. Significant progress has been made in recent years to strengthen the independence and competence of the courts and to combat corruption in the judiciary. Nonetheless, several important issues still need to be addressed, such as lengthy court proceedings, lack of funds and personnel able to deal with the increasing number of cases.

[420] Romanian courts are not always prepared to deal with the sophisticated contractual provisions that are sometimes found in mergers and acquisition transactions. Enforcement of such provisions in court can prove to be a cumbersome and time-consuming process. For this reason, in many complex transactions, international arbitration is chosen as the appropriate dispute resolution mechanism.

13 MERGER CONTROLS: ANTITRUST/ COMPETITION ISSUES

13.1 Relevant Legislation and Competent Authorities

[421] The merger control regime in Romania is regulated by the following main legislative enactments:

- law no. 21/1996 on competition (the '*Competition Law*'), as republished;
- the 2017 Merger Control Regulation (the '*2017 Merger Regulation*'), approved by Order of the Competition Council's President no. 431/2017;
- the Guidelines on the concepts of economic concentration, undertakings concerned, full-functionality and turnover, approved by Order of the Competition Council's President no. 386/2010;
- the Guidelines on restrictions directly related to and necessary for the implementation of economic concentrations (the '*Ancillary Restraints Guidelines*'), approved by Order of the Competition Council's President no. 387/2010;
- the Guidelines on the calculation of the authorization fee for economic concentrations, approved by Order of the Competition Council's President no. 439/2016; and
- the Guidelines on commitments applicable in the case of economic concentrations, approved by Order of the Competition Council's President no. 688/2010.

[422] The RCC is the national competition authority competent to control and authorize economic concentrations in Romania (in Romanian, *Consiliul Concurenței*, with the official website at www.consiliulconcurentei.ro). The RCC is a member of the European Competition Network (ECN) and the International Competition Network (ICN).

[423] The RCC is the national competition authority involved in the control of economic concentrations of a national dimension. In the event that the CEISD, in charge of the FDI screening, communicates to the RCC that a notified economic concentration operation is likely to present risks for national security, the merger control deadlines are suspended from the date of this communication.

[424] Economic concentrations that have a 'Community Dimension' must be notified, prior to their implementation, to the European Commission pursuant to the procedure provided under the EU Merger Regulation.

13.2 Notification

[425] Economic concentrations falling within the criteria and thresholds dictated by the Competition Law must be notified to the RCC. A concentration must be notified to the RCC after the conclusion of the agreement based on which control is to be acquired but before its implementation. It is possible to submit the notification before the conclusion of the agreement, upon demonstrating the parties' good faith intention to conclude the transaction or, in the case where the acquisition takes place by way of a public offer after having announced the intention of making such an offer.

[426] Under the Competition Law, clearance from the RCC must be obtained prior to the implementation of an economic concentration. Until the RCC clears the transaction, there is a mandatory standstill obligation before the transaction may be lawfully implemented.

[427] As an exception, the RCC has the right to grant a derogation from the non-implementation rule based on a reasoned request received from the parties. However, in practice, the RCC has approved few derogations and only in exceptional circumstances (e.g., financial and economic distress of the target undertaking, potential risk of losing part of the business).

13.3 Scope of the Controls

[428] Under the Competition Law, a concentration is deemed to arise where a change of control on a lasting basis results from:

(a) the merger of two or more previously independent undertakings or parts of undertakings;

(b) the acquisition, by one or more persons already controlling at least one undertaking, or by one or more undertakings, whether by the purchase of securities or assets, by contract or by other means, of direct or indirect control of the whole or parts of one or more other undertakings; *or*

(c) the creation of a joint venture performing on a lasting basis all the functions of an autonomous economic entity (a 'full-function' joint venture).

[429] Control is defined as the power to exercise a decisive influence over another undertaking. Decisive influence represents the power to determine the strategic commercial behaviour of an undertaking on the market (e.g., appointment of its board of directors, approval of its budget or business plan, entry into a new product or geographical markets). Control may be acquired by various means, such as acquisition of shares, veto rights and the power to appoint more than half of the board members. Control can also be exercised on a de facto basis.

[430] Notification is required for a merger, acquisition or joint venture where:

(a) the combined worldwide turnover of the parties involved for the previous financial year (or, if they are part of a group of companies, the combined turnover of the respective groups) exceeds the RON equivalent of EUR10 m; *and*

(b) the turnover of each of at least two of the parties involved (or, if they are part of a group of companies, the turnover of the respective groups), derived from activities carried out in Romania, exceeds the RON equivalent of EUR4 m.

[431] The RON equivalent is calculated at the official exchange rate published on 31 December by the National Bank of Romania for the year preceding the transaction date.

[432] The turnover represents the income resulting from the sale of products and/or provision of services in the year preceding notification. There are specific rules for determining the undertakings concerned and their groups, the concept of turnover and rules for its calculation, and for the geographical allocation of turnover, among others. The turnover must be adjusted according to several rules prescribed by the RCC, the most important being that intragroup turnover, any taxes directly related to the sale of products and/or the provision of services (e.g., excise duties) and export values (including intra-community deliveries) must be excluded.

[433] Foreign-to-foreign mergers and the acquisition or creation of full-function joint ventures must also be notified if the transaction meets the relevant notification thresholds.

[434] The Competition Law provides several exceptions to the above rule, where even though the jurisdictional thresholds are met, clearance is not required. The following operations are not considered economic concentrations:

- banks and other credit and financial institutions, insurance and reinsurance companies – the normal activities of which include transactions and dealing in securities for their own account or for the account of others – which

acquire securities on a temporary basis for resale, provided that they do not exercise voting rights in respect of those securities to determine the competitive behaviour of that undertaking or provided that they exercise such voting rights only to prepare the disposal of those securities and that any such disposal takes place within one year of the date of acquisition (the RCC may extend the one-year term);
- control is acquired by a liquidator appointed by a court decision or by another person mandated by a public authority to pursue proceedings related to the cessation of payments, judicial liquidation or any other similar proceedings;
- restructuring and reorganizing transactions within the same group of undertakings (intragroup operations);
- the acquisition of control is made by an undertaking – the sole business purpose of which is to acquire, manage and dispose of the respective participations – without involvement in the management of that controlled undertaking and without exercising the voting rights in respect of that controlled undertaking, in particular, in relation to the appointment of the management and supervisory bodies of the controlled undertaking, except where only to maintain the full value of such investment, but not to determine directly or indirectly the competitive conduct of the controlled undertaking.

13.4 Process/Mechanics

[435] The prior notification and clearance of an economic concentration that meets the turnover thresholds in the Competition Law are mandatory, and the concentration cannot be implemented before the RCC has cleared the transaction. Both pre-notification of prospective deals and post-deal notification of concluded deals follow the same procedural steps as described below.

[436] Within the pre-notification phase, both formal and informal guidance can be obtained from the RCC before the actual submission of the notification. Based on a pre-agreement or other binding agreements, pre-notification meetings or discussions can be organized with the case team allocated by the RCC. Such meetings are advisable in order to clarify any aspects regarding the notification and the overall process.

[437] Following the pre-notification phase, the parties to the concentration submit the formal notification of the economic concentration to the RCC. Pursuant to the law, the undertaking acquiring control has the obligation to notify the RCC. In practice, this means that:

- in the case of mergers, each of the merging undertakings must notify;
- in an acquisition of sole or joint control, the acquirer(s) must notify; and
- where a full-function joint venture is created, the undertakings which will hold joint control must notify.

13.5 Procedure for Assessment and Approval/Rejection of Deals

[438] Within seven days following submission of the notification, the RCC informs the parties in writing whether the notification file meets (from a formal perspective) the requirements to be deemed validly submitted.

[439] Submission of a complete notification form triggers phase I of the procedure. The RCC has twenty days to request additional information if it considers that the notification form is incomplete (the parties must respond no later than fifteen days after receipt of the additional request for information from the RCC). There may be several rounds of requests for information/answers until a notification is deemed complete by the RCC.

[440] The notification becomes effective as of the date the RCC considers that the information received is both accurate and complete. The RCC must immediately inform the notifying parties in respect of the date when the notification has become effective.

[441] In addition, upon receiving a notification of an economic concentration, the RCC will publish on its website and/or in the press a note regarding the notified operation. The note will identify the undertakings concerned, their country of origin, the nature of the concentration, the economic sectors concerned and the date when the RCC received the notification. However, the parties can request (providing sound reasons) that no publication be made until the issuance of the final decision.

[442] Within forty-five days from the effective date, the RCC must either issue a non-objection decision (subject to conditions where appropriate) or order the initiation of an in-depth investigation if it believes that the economic concentration may significantly impede competition (phase II). If the RCC does not issue a decision within the above term, the concentration is considered authorised.

[443] However, where the RCC decides to initiate an investigation, proceeding to phase II of the procedure, it will analyse the compatibility of the economic concentration with the competition environment.

[444] At the end of the investigation, the RCC can issue:

- a refusal decision;
- an authorization decision; or
- a conditional authorization decision.

[445] The investigation must be completed within five months from the effective date. If the RCC does not issue a decision within this term, the concentration is considered authorised.

[446] At the end of the procedure, the decisions of the RCC are published on its website. The parties are asked before publication to identify the confidential information in the decision which should not be published and to provide reasons as to why confidentiality is requested.

[447] In the case that the RCC intends to accept remedies/undertakings proposed by the parties, it will publish a summary of the case and contents of the proposed remedies, and any interested third parties can send their observations within the terms set by the RCC.

[448] For an overview of the main procedural steps of the RCC's assessment of economic concentrations, please refer to the illustration below.

14 ROMANIA: MERGER NOTIFICATION PROCEDURE

[449] The law provides for mandatory periods within which the RCC must issue a decision in respect of the notified economic concentration, failing which the economic concentration will be deemed authorized upon elapse of the relevant term (i.e., forty-five days or five months from the date when notification of the economic concentration became effective, for phase I or phase II procedures, respectively).

[450] Since phase I and phase II periods only start from the date when the notification becomes effective, the procedure may be significantly delayed, effectively depending on how quickly the notifying parties provide the information required by the RCC.

[451] However, certain steps may be taken to speed up the procedure, such as:

- pre-notification discussions may be initiated with the RCC at least two weeks prior to the intended date of submission of a notification;
- the notification may be submitted based on pre-agreement confirming the intended transactions (e.g., memorandum of understanding, letter of intent);
- proposing remedies during phase I of the procedure if a conditional clearance is anticipated; and
- proactively liaising with the RCC case team (through meetings and discussions) in order to clarify aspects related to the notification. This usually happens in practice, through meetings with the case team both prior to and after submission of the notification and is very helpful in speeding up the procedure.

14.1 What Deals Are Likely to Be Refused/Rejected?

[452] The substantive test applied by the RCC in merger control proceedings is whether a concentration leads to significant impediments to effective competition on the Romanian market or a substantial part thereof (SIEC test), in particular by creating or strengthening a dominant position on the Romanian market or a part thereof (under Romanian law dominance is presumed at a market share of 40% or more).

[453] In its assessment of economic concentrations, the RCC will consider a broad set of criteria, including the market position of the parties and the degree of concentration on the relevant market(s), entry barriers (regulatory, financial or otherwise), the position of actual or potential competitors and the extent to which other competitive constraints exist in order to limit the market power of the undertaking(s) concerned.

[454] However, in assessing the compatibility of an economic concentration with competition law, the RCC will also consider economic efficiency criteria to the benefit of consumers (e.g., reduction of costs and prices, increasing the innovation on the market or improvement of supply and technical progress) to which the concentration may lead.

[455] The analysis of the RCC focuses on the level of concentration on the market (and the likelihood of an increase in the market share of the parties) but also on the effects on prices (and the likelihood of the concentration leading to higher prices). The RCC uses economic analysis (e.g., the Upward Pricing Pressure test for analysis of unilateral effects in horizontal mergers, which consists of identifying the incentives of firms to raise prices post-merger by comparing the upward pricing pressure due to loss in competition and the opposing downward pricing pressure exerted due to cost synergies).

[456] Lastly, it is important to note that the Competition Law and GEO 46/2022 provide for the right of the Romanian Government to issue a decision prohibiting the acquisition of control over undertakings or assets or the planned foreign investment (even for below-control acquisitions planned by EU or Romanian nationals), upon a proposal from the CEISD, where the operation poses risks to national security, public order or projects or programmes of EU interest. However, based on publicly available information, no such prohibition decision has been issued to date and there is no clear definition of the cases and criteria which may give rise to national security or public order risks.

14.2 Views of Third Parties

[457] The RCC may ask for and take into account the views of third parties or other stakeholders in the assessment of economic concentrations.

[458] To this end, the RCC may ask any third parties to provide information and documents which it considers relevant in the assessment of the concentration, including through interviews (provided the person concerned agrees to be interviewed), questionnaires addressed to third parties such as suppliers, customers, competitors or trade associations and meetings with representatives of the undertakings concerned.

[459] In practice, the RCC publishes on its website an invitation for third parties to submit comments in respect of economic concentrations that are under analysis. The RCC may also ask third parties to submit their comments when it intends to accept commitments proposed by the undertakings concerned.

14.3 Possible Remedies

[460] If an economic concentration has the potential to adversely affect competition on the Romanian market or a substantial part thereof, the parties may propose remedies which address the anticompetitive concerns and make the concentration compatible with a normal competitive environment.

[461] The Competition Law allows both behavioural and structural remedies. However, in theory, structural remedies are preferred due to their likelihood to better address the competition issues raised by the concentration and the ability of the RCC to monitor their compliance. Possible remedies include divestments of assets and/or activities which may be operated separately, termination or amendment of existing exclusive agreements and granting access to necessary infrastructure, networks or key technologies.

[462] The proposed remedies must be sufficient to eliminate all the competition concerns identified by the RCC and must be complete, efficient and capable of being enforced in a timely manner.

14.4 Approvals in the Context of a Bid for a Publicly Held Company

[463] Public offers or series of dealings with publicly listed securities whereby control is acquired from different sellers may be carried out subject to the condition that the relevant concentration is notified without delay to the RCC and that the acquired voting rights are not exercised unless such is necessary for preserving the investment and conditional upon an express derogation granted by the RCC (and that no other implementation acts are taken prior to the decision clearing the transaction).

[464] Aside from the above, the timing of approvals is the same, meaning forty-five days for phase I and five months for phase II from the date when the notification of the economic concentration became effective.

14.5 Potential Sanctions

[465] The RCC may impose severe sanctions for breaching the merger control or other antitrust laws.

[466] Failure to notify an economic concentration prior to its implementation can be sanctioned with an administrative fine between 0.5% and 10% of the total turnover of the infringing undertaking(s) during the year preceding the year of the sanctioning decision.

[467] Where a concentration has been implemented, and it is subsequently prohibited, the RCC may request that the concentration be reversed (e.g., by dissolution of the merger or new entity resulting from the concentration, the disposal of the shares or the acquired assets) or may impose any other measures adequate to restore the situation prevailing before the concentration.

[468] Failure to comply with the conditions or measures imposed by a decision of the RCC may be subject to an administrative fine between 0.5% and 10% of the total turnover of the infringing undertaking during the year preceding the year of the sanctioning decision.

[469] Providing incomplete, inaccurate or misleading information to the RCC may result in an administrative fine between 0.1% and 1% of the total turnover of the infringing undertaking(s) during the year preceding the year of the sanctioning decision.

[470] Breach of antitrust rules, such as an abuse of a dominant position or agreements or concerted practices which have as their object or effect the restriction, prevention or distortion of competition on the Romanian market, are sanctioned with an administrative fine between 0.5% and 10% of the total turnover of the infringing undertaking during the year preceding the year of the sanctioning decision.

14.6 Anticompetitive Restraints

[471] Economic concentrations often involve certain restrictions which are directly related and necessary for the respective concentration to be effectively implemented by the parties, also known as 'ancillary restraints'.

[472] According to the Ancillary Restraints Guidelines, such restrictions include non-compete, non-solicitation and confidentiality obligations, as well as other types of restrictions necessary for the effective implementation of an economic concentration, such as licence agreements (where the vendor retains ownership over the IPR connected to the assets and know-how transferred) or obligations of supply (usually agreed between the vendor and the buyer for a transitory period, where this is necessary for the effective operation of the business transferred).

[473] A clearance decision of an economic concentration by the RCC will generally also cover those restrictions, provided they are directly related and necessary to the relevant concentration. However, the undertakings concerned must assess for themselves whether and to what extent the restraints are ancillary to the economic concentration.

14.7 Limitations on the Permissible Duration and/or Geographical Scope of Restraints

[474] As concerns duration, non-compete, non-solicitation and confidentiality obligations will be considered ancillary to the concentration provided they are limited to a maximum of three years when the transfer of the undertaking includes the transfer of customer loyalty in the form of both goodwill and know-how, and a maximum of two years when only goodwill is included. A longer duration is permitted in the case of full-function joint ventures.

[475] The geographical area where such restrictions may apply can only cover the areas where the vendor offered the relevant products and/or services prior to the transfer. Exceptionally, areas which the vendor intended to penetrate (provided it also made investments for this specific purpose) may be covered by the ancillary restraints.

[476] The object of the ancillary restraints will be limited to those services and products which formed the scope of activity of the transferred undertaking prior to the concentration.

14.8 Preventing the Departure of the Management Team and/or Key Employees

[477] From a legal perspective, it is not generally possible to prevent employees (the management team and/or key employees) from departing from a company. However, several legal provisions under Law no. 11/1991 on the prohibition of unfair competition, as subsequently republished (the '*Unfair Competition Law*') and under Law no. 53/2003 regarding the Romanian labour code, as subsequently republished and amended (the '*Labour Code*') aid in limiting the negative impact of a potential loss of key personnel following the implementation of a concentration.

[478] Under the Unfair Competition Law, diverting the clients of an undertaking by a former or current employee/representative or by any other person by using trade secrets for the protection of which the respective undertaking had taken reasonable protection measures and the disclosure of which could damage the interests of such undertaking is prohibited. Moreover, Government Emergency Ordinance no. 25/2019 on the protection of know-how and undisclosed business information amounting to trade secrets against the acquisition, use and illegal disclosure ('*GEO 25/2019*') prohibits using or disclosing a trade secret if done without the consent of the trade secret's owner by a person who fulfils any of the following conditions: (i) it acquired the trade secret illegally, (ii) it is in breach of a confidentiality agreement or any other obligation of not disclosing the trade secret, or (iii) it is in breach of an obligation of a contractual or other nature limiting the use of the trade secret. Protection under the Unfair Competition Law and GEO 25/2019 is, however, limited due to a lack of effective sanctions (i.e., small administrative fines).

[479] Pursuant to the provisions of the Labour Code, employees may be restricted in performing competing activities in their own interest or in the interest of a third party, after termination of employment with the employer. Such obligations which are generally provided in the labour agreement are optional, negotiable and subject to express validity conditions – for example, the employer cannot completely prevent the employee from practising his or her profession or specialization, the clause is subject to payment by the employer of a minimum compensation throughout the duration of the non-compete obligations amounting to 50% of the employee's average gross salary, during the last six months of employment, the duration of the non-compete obligations is of maximum two years from the termination of employment, the geographic area covered by the non-compete clause cannot exceed the area where the employee can be in real competition with the employer.

[480] An employer may also ask an employee to accept a confidentiality clause in his/her employment contract. Under such clause, the employer shall be entitled to ask the employee not to disclose data or information the employee acquired during his or her term of employment and after its termination.

14.9 Constraints Affecting Competitive Behaviour after the Deal Has Been Implemented

[481] After an economic concentration has been implemented, a company must comply with the competition rules which prohibit non-exempted agreements or concerted practices which have as their object or effect the restriction, prevention or distortion of competition on the Romanian market.

[482] Also, in cases of dominance (usually above 40% market share), an undertaking must not abuse its dominant position through practices such as discrimination, margin squeeze and refusal to deal.

[483] EU block exemption regulations also apply to agreements, concerted practices and/or decisions by associations of undertakings under national competition law.

14.10 The Relevant Competition Authorities

[484] The RCC is the relevant public authority which is charged with enforcing competition rules in Romania and has proved to be quite effective in practice. Recent actions taken by the RCC include the sanctioning of undertakings with high fines in a number of cartels, abuse of dominance cases, as well as some vertical agreements.

[485] The RCC is also active in monitoring (either directly or through an appointed third party) remedies undertaken by the parties, as well as the impact of economic concentrations on the relevant markets.

15 TAXATION ASPECTS

15.1 Liability to Tax

[486] The following business entities are liable to pay CIT in Romania:

- Romanian legal entities;
- legal entities incorporated in accordance with the EU legislation and having their registered seat in Romania;

- non-resident legal entities performing activities in Romania through one or more permanent establishments, with respect to the profit attributable to the permanent establishment/s;
- foreign legal entities which have the place of effective management in Romania;
- foreign legal entities which obtain income from or in connection to real estate located in Romania or from the transfer of participation titles held in a Romanian legal entity.

[487] A non-resident company is considered tax resident in Romania also, in case it has its *place of effective management* in Romania. The place of effective management represents the place where a non-resident entity carries out operations corresponding to economic, real, and substantial purposes in case one of the following conditions is fulfilled:

- the economic–strategic decisions necessary for the management of the non-resident entity are taken in Romania by the executive directors or members of the board of directors;
- at least 50% of the executive directors or members of the board of directors of the non-resident entity are residents therein.

15.2 Taxation of Permanent Establishments

[488] A permanent establishment is deemed to be a fixed place of business where a non-resident carries out its activity either directly or through a dependent agent.

[489] Non-resident legal entities which carry out activities in Romania through a permanent establishment are subject to profit tax in Romania in relation to the taxable profit allocated to the respective permanent establishment, in accordance with the 2010 OECD Report on the Attribution of Profits to Permanent Establishments.

[490] Also, permanent establishments carrying out taxable operations in the territory of Romania might have the obligation to register for VAT purposes in Romania and, consequently, to comply with the reporting and payment requirements provided by the VAT legislation.

[491] Moreover, non-resident legal entities which carry out activities in Romania through several permanent establishments must appoint one of these permanent establishments to fulfil the declarative obligations for all the permanent establishments registered in Romania. For this purpose, all income and expenses pertaining to the other permanent establishments of the relevant non-resident entity are aggregated at the level of the appointed permanent establishment.

15.2.1 Corporate Income Tax

[492] Romanian legal entities are generally subject to the 16% profit tax rate in Romania with respect to their worldwide income. Nevertheless, relief may be granted in Romania in respect of foreign source income, depending on the applicable double tax treaty.

[493] Nightclubs, night bars, discos and casinos (inclusively legal entities that carry out these activities through a joint venture) shall pay the minimum tax between 5% of the revenues obtained from such activities and 16% of the taxable profit.

[494] Taxpayers with a turnover over EUR50 m from the previous year are required to pay the minimum between the corporate income tax and 1% of the turnover. Credit institutions (Romanian legal entities and branches in Romania of non-resident legal entities) are obliged to pay a turnover tax, in addition to the corporate income tax, at the rate of 2% applied on the turnover for the fiscal years 2024–2025 and 1% starting from 2026.

[495] During 2024 and 2025, legal entities operating in the oil and gas sector, with a turnover over EUR50 m in the previous year, will be subject to a specific turnover tax of 0.5% on the adjusted turnover, in addition to the corporate income tax. Taxpayers exclusively engaged in the distribution, supply or transport of electricity and natural gas, subject to ANRE regulations, are exempt.

[496] Microenterprises are subject to a tax on revenues, the following tax rates being applicable:

(i) 1% applicable for microenterprises that obtain revenues below EUR60 000 inclusively and do not obtain revenues according to the NACE codes mentioned below.

(ii) 3% applicable for microenterprises that obtain revenues exceeding EUR60 000 or that carry-out activities corresponding to the following NACE codes related to software development activities, HoReCa, legal assistance, medical and dental assistance: 5832, 5829, 6201, 6209, 5510, 5520, 5530, 5590, 5610, 5621, 5629, 5630, 6910, 8621, 8622, 8623, 8690.

(iii) A micro-company is a Romanian legal entity which cumulatively fulfils the following conditions on 31 December of the previous year:

- its annual turnover is lower than the RON equivalent of EUR500 000;
- its shares are held by entities other than the state or local authorities; and
- it is not in undergoing dissolution/liquidation proceedings registered with the trade registry/judicial courts;
- the revenues from consulting and/or management (with the exception of tax consultancy services related to NACE code 6920) must not exceed 20% of total revenues;
- has shareholders who hold directly or indirectly more than 25% of the value/number of shares, and it is the single entity appointed by the shareholders to apply the microenterprise tax regime;
- has at least one full-time employee;
- timely submitted the financial statements.

15.2.2 Disposal of Shares

[497] Capital gains obtained by Romanian or foreign entities from the disposal, valuation or revaluation of shares held in a Romanian or foreign legal entity are subject to the standard corporate income tax rate of 16%. However, the Romanian tax legislation also provides an exemption in case the taxpayer holds at least 10% of the share capital of the company in which it has the shares for an interrupted period of at least one year.

[498] Mergers, spin-offs (representing a transfer of a branch of activity) and transfers of assets in certain conditions, respectively, share swaps between Romanian companies or between a Romanian company and a foreign company, are not subject to tax.

15.2.3 Value Added Tax

[499] As of 1 January 2017, the standard Romanian VAT rate is 19% and applies to all supplies of goods and services, including imports, which do not benefit from an exemption or from the VAT reduced rates referred to below.

[500] Reduced VAT rates (5% and 9%) apply for deliveries of certain goods or services, as follows:

- 9% – applied to accommodation, restaurants and catering services, certain foods, medicines for human and veterinary use, orthopaedic products, water for irrigation in agriculture, water supply and sewerage, fertilizers and pesticides used in agriculture, seeds and other agricultural products for sowing or planting, as well as specific categories of services in connection with agriculture, immovable properties in certain conditions, supply and installation of photovoltaic panels, access to sports events and amusement parks.
- 5% – applied to books, newspapers, magazines, access to museums, etc., and certain supplies of energy and firewood.

15.2.4 Taxes on Land Transactions

[501] Although no stamp duties are applied in Romania, land transactions must be performed, for validity purposes, only through notarized deeds, which are subject to notarization fees, in variable amounts computed pro rata with the value of the relevant land transaction.

15.2.5 Local Taxes

[502] There are specific taxes that are due to the local council (which are mainly related to property or certain activities). The most important are listed below.

Taxes on Buildings and Land

Buildings

[503] The building tax computation method is dependent on the destination usage of the building as such:

- Residential buildings: Tax rate between 0.08% and 0.2% (applicable to the taxable value as per the specific table provided by the law for individuals and the value resulting from the evaluation report for legal entities).
- Non-residential buildings: Tax rate between 0.2% and 1.3%. In the case of a building used for agricultural purposes, the applicable tax rate is 0.4%.

[504] For legal entities who did not perform a revaluation of the building during the last five years, the tax on the building is 5%.

[505] Building tax is paid annually, in two equal instalments, by 31 March and 30 September; the building tax may be subject to a reduction of up to 10% if it is paid in full prior to 31 March.

[506] Individuals who own residential buildings located in Romania whose taxable value exceeds RON2 500 000 will be additionally taxed at a rate of 0.3% applied to the difference between its taxable value and this threshold. The tax must be declared and paid by 30 April of the current fiscal year.

[507] A new taxation system may be applied starting with 1 January 2025. The specific legislation was published at the end of 2022 and was envisaged to be applicable starting with 2023, but afterwards, its applicability was postponed until 2025.

[508] Under the envisaged system, the tax on buildings and the lands underneath will be determined based on a taxable value determined by the Local Authority using the estimated values provided by the National Union of the Public Notaries in Romania (the latter will perform benchmark studies on the estimated values of real estate in Romania).

[509] The taxable value of the buildings is determined by the square metre of the built-up area of a building multiplied by the value/square metre established by these studies.

[510] The tax rates to be applied are at least the following (it represents the minimum tax rate that can be increased by a maximum of 50% by each Local Authority, depending on their decision):

- 0.1% for residential buildings;
- 0.5% for non-residential buildings.

Land

[511] Landowners are subject to local land tax established at a fixed amount per square metre, depending on the rank of the locality where the land is located and the area and category of land use, pursuant to the classifications made by local councils.

[512] The tax on land is paid annually, in two equal instalments, by 31 March and 30 September; the building tax may be subject to a reduction of up to 10% if it is paid in full prior to 31 March.

Tax on Vehicles

[513] Any person owning a vehicle registered in Romania is subject to an annual tax, depending on the vehicle type.

[514] Individuals/legal entities owning cars registered in Romania with a purchase value of more than RON375 000 will be additionally taxed at a rate of 0.3% applied on the difference between the purchase value and the threshold. The tax is due for a period of five years starting from the year of delivery -receipt of the car and is payable until 31 December of the current fiscal year.

Tax for Issuing Building Permits and Related Approvals, as well as Other Types of Permits Issued by Local Authorities

[515] Any person who needs approval or specific authorization from a local council in Romania is subject to a specific local tax.

Tax on Displays for Advertising and Publicity Purposes

[516] Any person using a panel display or a display structure for advertising and publicity must pay an annual tax to the local budget of the village, town or city in the area where the panel, display or other display structure is located.

[517] The amount is computed annually by multiplying the number of square metres or fraction of a square metre of display area for advertising or publicity with the amount determined by the local council.

15.2.6 Capital Duties or Other Duties on Share Capital

[518] No capital duties or other duties on share capital are applicable in Romania.

15.2.7 Business Rates

[519] No business rates are applicable in Romania.

15.2.8 Taxes Imposed on Employers (E.g., Pay-As-You-Earn (PAYE) Tax and Social Security Obligations)

[520] As a general rule, employment income realized in Romania is subject to personal income tax of 10% and social contributions (certain exemptions apply pursuant to the provisions of the EU regulations on the coordination of social security systems or pursuant to the social security agreements signed between Romania and non-EEA countries).

[521] The social contribution rates are due to both the employers and the employees. The currently applicable social contribution rates are as follows:

Employer Contributions:

- work insurance contribution: 2.25%;
- pensions fund social security contribution: 4%, 8% depending on working conditions.

Employee Contributions:

- pensions fund social security contribution: 25%;
- health contribution: 10%.

[522] For the purpose of declaring and paying the payroll taxes, employers and entities similar to employers must file a single tax return.

[523] Employers compute and withhold salary taxes by the 25th of the month following the month when the salary income was obtained.

[524] As of 1 November 2023, the following tax incentives shall be granted for the salary income earned by individuals from employers acting in the field of construction:

- Personal income tax is not due for gross income up to and including RON10 000; for the part exceeding this amount, income tax of 10% is due.
- Social security contribution is 21.25%, applied only for gross income up to and including RON10 000; for the part exceeding this threshold, social security contribution of 25% is due.

15.2.9 Customs and Excise Duties

[525] Customs duties are established in Romania in compliance with the EU Common Customs Tariff.

[526] Customs duties are expressed as a percentage applied to the customs value or as a fixed amount applied to a specific quantity. Agricultural products are subject to specific customs duties.

[527] With regard to the excise duties, Romania complies with the EU law on harmonized excise duties involving strict rules and conditions to be observed by economic operators. The following products are subject to harmonized excise duties:

- alcohol and alcoholic beverages;
- processed tobacco; and
- energy products (e.g., gasoline, diesel, gas, coal) and electricity.

[528] Excise duties are due in the Member State of consumption when excise goods are released for consumption (e.g., extraction, production, importation thereof, or release from an excise duty suspension regime).

[529] Production of excisable goods is subject to obtaining a fiscal warehouse authorization. In the production, no retail sales are allowed, except in certain cases expressly provided by the law.

[530] Storage tax warehouses are allowed for energy products, processed tobacco, as well as for ethyl alcohol and alcoholic beverages, and the excise duties become chargeable at the time when the products are released from consumption (are dispatched from the fiscal warehouse).

[531] Traders who sell, either wholesale or retail, energy products (gasoline, diesel, kerosene, liquefied petroleum gas and biofuels), as well as those who distribute and sell alcoholic beverages and/or processed tobacco, in wholesale but which are not tax warehouse keepers, may carry out these operations only after obtaining a certificate for distribution and sale in the wholesale/retail system for these products.

[532] Besides the excise duties harmonized at the level of all EU Member States, the local legislation in Romania also provides non-harmonized excise duties applicable to products derived from heated tobacco and liquids containing nicotine, which are used for electronic cigarettes.

[533] Excise duties are generally payable by the 25th of the month following the chargeability.

[534] Exemptions from excise duties are available for specific excisable products intended for particular uses, for instance, energy products used in mineralogical processes or green electricity.

[535] The level of excise duties (excluding excise duties for cigarettes) is updated annually by the rate of inflation in the previous twelve months, calculated in September of the year before the new rates apply, and is published every year on the website of the Ministry of Finance no later than 31 December.

15.3 Incentives in Respect of Capital Expenditure

[536] Capital expenditure may benefit from various incentives pursuant to the Romanian Fiscal Code, as follows.

15.3.1 Fiscal Depreciation

[537] Romanian tax legislation provides a distinction between fiscal and accounting depreciation in terms of applicable tax treatment. The accounting depreciation represents non-deductible expenses, while the fiscal depreciation is considered a deductible expense for corporate income tax purposes.

[538] Expenses related to the purchase, production, construction, as well as improvement of depreciable fixed assets are recovered fiscally through fiscal depreciation.

A depreciable fixed asset is a tangible asset fulfilling the following cumulative conditions: (i) it is owned and used in the production, delivery of goods or the supply of services, for lease to third parties or for administrative purposes; (ii) its fiscal value is equal or exceeds a certain limit established through Government Decision; and (iii) it has a normal useful life exceeding one year.

[539] Fiscal depreciation is to be computed based on the asset's fiscal value and useful life for tax purposes by applying one of the permitted depreciation methods:

- straight-line method;
- accelerated depreciation; and
- reducing balance method.

[540] The useful lives to be considered for tax purposes are provided in the Fixed Asset Register.

[541] Under the Fiscal Code, machinery and equipment, tools and plant, computers and their peripherals, as well as patents, may benefit from the accelerated depreciation method, pursuant to which a maximum of 50% of the asset's fiscal value may be deducted during the first year of usage, while the rest of the asset's value can be depreciated using the straight-line method over its remaining useful life.

15.3.2 Expenses Related to Research and Development

[542] Entities subject to profit tax can benefit from an additional deduction of 50% of the eligible expenses for research and development. Moreover, accelerated depreciation may be applied for devices and equipment used in research and development activities. The conditions necessary to be able to apply the incentive are for the research to be relevant to the taxpayer's activity and to be performed in Romania or in the EU/EEA Member States.

[543] The newly incorporated taxpayers that perform exclusively innovation, research and development activities, as defined by Government Ordinance 57/2002 regarding the scientific research and technological development, as amended, as well as the related activities, are exempt from CIT for the first ten years of activity. In the case of taxpayers already set up at the date when this provision entered into force (6 January 2017), the CIT exemption is applicable for a period of ten years starting with this date (6 January 2017).

15.3.3 Tax Holiday for Reinvested Profit

[544] Tax holiday for profit reinvested in production/purchase of certain technological equipment (i.e., machinery, tools, installations provided in subgroup 2.1 and 2.2.9 of the Catalogue on the Classification and Normal Usage Life of Fixed Assets) and IT software, used for the purpose of carrying out economic activity benefits from profit tax exemption.

[545] The above profit tax exemption is applicable only in relation to new technological equipment (an asset is new if it was not used before the acquisition date) and only within the limit of the profit tax due for the tax period when the equipment has been put into use. That part of the profit that benefits from tax relief cannot be distributed to shareholders as a dividend; it must be left at the company's disposal as a reserve, subject to tax at the moment when the destination is changed.

[546] Also, taxpayers benefiting from the above incentive are obliged to keep in their own patrimony the respective technological equipment for a period of at least half of its economic useful life established in accordance with the applicable accounting regulation, but not more than five years.

[547] Moreover, the relevant taxpayers cannot apply the accelerated depreciation with respect to the technological equipment benefiting from this tax exemption on the reinvested profit.

15.4 Tax Consolidation

[548] Two or more Romanian companies can apply the CIT consolidation regime if they are held directly and indirectly in a percentage of at least 75% for an uninterrupted period of at least one year before the consolidated group for fiscal purposes enters existence. Additionally, the participants should also meet the following requirements:

- be exclusively corporate income taxpayers;
- have the same fiscal year;
- not be part of another tax group in the field of corporate taxation;
- not be in liquidation/ dissolution.

[549] Each member of the fiscal group has the obligation to prepare the transfer pricing file for the intragroup transactions carried out.

[550] In case a member of the consolidated group no longer fulfils the required conditions before the established period of five years, it leaves the tax group and no longer applies the consolidation system starting from the quarter following the one in which the conditions are no longer met. As such, the respective member has the obligation to recompute the profit tax on an individual basis for the period going forward and also for the period in which he was part of the group.

[551] Moreover, the responsible member has the obligation to recompute the tax result of the Group for the period between the commencement of the CIT consolidation and up to the quarter in which the conditions were not fulfilled. Therefore, the responsible member must submit rectifying statements for the said period.

[552] The obligation to recompute the CIT due is not applicable in the following cases:

- sale/ assignment of shares held by one of the group members, under the conditions that following this operation, the holding falls below 25% of the value/ number of shares or voting rights;
- the dissolution of a member of the group;
- the exit of a member of the group as a result of a reorganization procedure (i.e., merger, partial or total spin-off, transfer of assets, share exchanges).

[553] Moreover, in case all members of the group request the dissolution of the group during the fiscal year before the five-year period ends, the group is dissolved starting with the following fiscal year. Furthermore, in case the conditions for establishing the CIT group are no longer fulfilled, the group is dissolved. Under such circumstances, each member has the obligation to recompute the CIT due for the period during which the CIT group existed.

[554] From the VAT perspective, Romanian legal independent companies having a close bond in organizational, financial and economic terms have the possibility to consolidate their VAT results under a fiscal unique group subject to certain conditions.

15.5 CFC Rules

[555] In the case of a controlled company or a controlled permanent establishment (PE), the profit taxpayer controlling the said company or the said PE shall include in the tax base the undistributed income arising from interests, royalties, dividends, leases and insurances. The taxpayer will deduct the tax paid by the controlled entity/PE in the foreign state.

[556] An exemption from the consolidation of the income registered by controlled foreign is applicable as of January 2019, if the controlled foreign company meets cumulatively the following conditions:

- The controlled foreign company has its fiscal residence in a Member State of the EU or in a third-party member of the Economic European Area.
- The controlled foreign company carries out significant economic activities, supported by employees, equipment, assets and locations, as demonstrated by the relevant facts and circumstances.

15.6 Tax Considerations Arising on M&A Transactions

15.6.1 Mergers and Other Business Restructuring

[557] The Romanian tax law fully transposed the provisions of the European Directive 2009/133/CE regarding the common system of taxation applicable to mergers, divisions, transfers of assets and exchanges of shares concerning companies of different Member States (the '*Merger Directive*'). Most of these provisions apply to the business restructuring operations defined by the Directive performed between local companies.

[558] Consequently, for CIT payers:

- a merger, spin-off or partial spin-off does not give rise to any taxation of capital gains computed by reference to the difference between the market values of the assets/liabilities transferred and their values for tax purposes;
- on a merger, spin-off or exchange of shares, the allotment of securities representing the capital of the receiving or acquiring company to a shareholder

of the transferring or acquired company in exchange for securities representing the capital of the latter company does not give rise to any taxation of the income, profits or capital gains of that shareholder;
- on a partial spin-off, the allotment to a shareholder of the transferring company of securities representing the capital of the receiving company does not give rise to any taxation of the income, profits or capital gains of that shareholder.

[559] A partial spin-off is considered tax neutral from a CIT perspective, provided that a line of business/activity is transferred.

[560] A line of business is defined as the total assets and liabilities of a legal entity's division, which, from an organizational point of view, qualifies as an independent business, meaning an entity that is able to function by its own means.

[561] Criteria that need to be cumulatively met in order to fulfil the independent nature of a business:

- The division should be an organizational structure distinct from other divisions of the transferor company.
- The division should independently operate as a whole under the normal conditions of its economic sector. Such criteria should be assessed by verifying the existence of its own customers, its own tangible and intangible assets, its own inventory, its own personnel, as well as other assets and liabilities that are indirectly linked to the transferred line of business. If the case, the division includes its own administrative services (e.g., accounting department and decentralized personnel service).
- The division should perform its activity at the moment when the transfer is approved by the general meetings of the companies, both the transferor and the transferee, or at the date when the transfer takes effect, if different.

[562] Furthermore, Methodological norms state that a line of business does not include:

- Assets or liabilities related to other divisions of the transferor.
- Assets or liabilities related to the management of the transferor.
- Insular assets or liabilities.

[563] In cases of business restructuring operations between local companies and CIT payers, the following rules are applicable:

- the transfer of assets and liabilities is not treated as a taxable transfer;
- the exchange of shares held in a Romanian legal entity for equity of another legal person is not treated as a taxable transfer;
- the distribution of shares in connection with the division of a Romanian legal person is not treated as a dividend;
- a transferred asset or liability has the same tax value at the person receiving that it had at the transferring company;
- tax depreciation of any transferred asset will continue to be calculated by the receiving company using the same rules as if the transfer had not taken place;

- transferring a provision or a reserve is not considered a reduction or cancellation of the provision or reserve if the receiving company takes them and maintains them at the value had before the transfer.

[564] Fiscal loss recorded by taxpayers who cease to exist as a result of a merger or division shall be recovered by the newly established taxpayers or by those that take over the assets of the company being acquired or divided, in proportion to the assets and liabilities transferred to legal persons benefiting, according to the merger/division project. Fiscal loss recorded by taxpayers that do not cease to exist as a result of a spin-off operation shall be to be recovered by these taxpayers, in proportion to the assets and liabilities maintained in their patrimony and by those that take over the assets, in proportion to the assets transferred to them.

15.6.2 Sale of Shares (For Cash, Shares or Other Securities)

From the Vendor's Perspective

Individual Vendor

[565] Capital gains generated in Romania by individuals are generally subject to the 10% income tax rate.

[566] The gain/loss resulting from the transfer of securities other than financial derivatives shall be the positive/negative difference between the selling price and the purchase price per type of securities, diminished, as the case may be, by the related costs of the transaction.

[567] The determination of gain/loss from the transfer of securities, other than financial derivative instruments, shall be carried out on the date of:

- conclusion of the transaction, based on supporting documents, by the intermediary as defined under the relevant legislation, Romanian tax resident, if the operation is carried out through an intermediary;
- making the payment of transaction price, based on supporting documents, by the beneficiary of income if the operation is not carried out through an intermediary or the intermediary is not a Romanian tax resident.

[568] The net annual gain/net annual loss shall be determined as the difference between gains and losses registered during the fiscal year, cumulated from the beginning of the year from the transfer of securities and any other operations with financial instruments, including financial derivatives instruments, as well as the transfer of financial gold, defined by the law.

[569] The net annual gain/net annual loss shall be determined by the taxpayer (beneficiary of the income) based on the Annual Statement regarding income tax and social charges due from taxpayers.

[570] The taxable annual net gain from the transfer of securities, from any other operations with financial instruments, including derivative financial instruments, as well as from the transfer of financial gold, shall be determined by the taxpayer as

the difference between the annual net gain and the losses carried over from the previous fiscal years resulting from these operations.

[571] Net annual loss resulting from the transfer of securities, determined by the Annual Statement regarding income tax and social charges due from taxpayers, can be carried forward for up to seven consecutive tax years against the profits having the same nature.

Legal entity

[572] The revenues obtained from the sale of shares held by a Romanian legal person or a foreign legal person located in a country with which Romania concluded a Double Tax Treaty are treated as non-taxable if, at the date of the sale, the vendor holds at least 10% of the share capital for an uninterrupted period of one year. This relief applies to both Romanian and foreign legal entities located in a country with which Romania concluded a Double Tax Treaty. Should the holding condition mentioned above not be met, the capital gains are taxable in Romania in the following cases:

- The vendor does not prove that it is resident in a country with which Romania concluded a Double Tax Treaty (does not provide a tax residency certificate).
- Romania did not conclude a Double Tax Treaty with the country where the vendor is a resident.
- Romania concluded a Double Tax Treaty with the country where the vendor is a resident, but the Double Tax Treaty gives taxation rights to Romania.

[573] In case the capital gains are taxable in Romania, the foreign vendor has the obligation to declare and pay CIT in Romania by registering for this purpose.

15.7 Determination of Values

[574] Values are freely negotiable between the parties, subject, however, to the following limitations.

15.7.1 Artificial Transactions

[575] When establishing the amount of a tax, the tax authorities are entitled to ignore a transaction which does not have an economic purpose or they may reclassify the transaction in order to reflect its economic purpose.

[576] If a transaction or a series of transactions are qualified as being artificial, they will not benefit from the more favourable provisions of the double tax treaties (artificial transactions are deemed to be those transactions/series of transactions which do not have an economic content and which may not be normally used within standard economic practices, their essential goal being that of avoiding taxation or of obtaining fiscal advantages which could not be granted otherwise).

15.7.2 Reference Value of Prices Established in Real Estate Transactions

[577] Income realized by individuals from real estate transactions is computed pro rata with the declared value of the relevant transaction.

[578] The income tax paid for the transfer of ownership is withheld by the notary public and calculated by applying a 3% tax rate on the value declared by the parties in the transfer documents.

[579] If the value declared by the parties (i.e., the transaction price) is lower than the estimated value determined as a result of an appraisal conducted by the Chamber of Notaries Public, the notary public notifies the tax authorities in relation to that specific transaction.

15.8 Transactions Between Related Parties

[580] Transactions between related parties must be performed at arm's length. Otherwise, the Romanian tax authorities are entitled to adjust the taxpayer's revenues or expenses in order to reflect the market value of a relevant transaction.

[581] Transactions with Romanian and non-resident related parties fall within the scope of the investigations regarding compliance with transfer pricing legislation.

[582] For the purpose of applying transfer pricing rules, Romanian tax authorities consider the OECD Transfer Pricing Guidelines.

15.9 Tax Reliefs, Exemptions or Deferrals for Restructuring and Reorganization

[583] No special rules apply with respect to tax reliefs, exemptions or deferrals on particular types of restructuring.

[584] Romania fully transposed the provisions of the Merger Directive into its local legislation and expanded them in relation to mergers and other business restructuring operations performed between local companies. Consequently, a merger, spin-off or other business restructuring operation as defined by the Directive will not be treated as a taxable event, and it should not give rise to a fiscal duty unless it is made for tax optimization only.

[585] It is possible to obtain advance tax clearances from the tax authorities in Romania prior to performing the relevant transactions. Companies may request an Advance Tax Ruling to this end to be issued by the National Agency for Fiscal Administration.

15.10 Carry Forward of Losses

[586] Companies are allowed to carry forward fiscal losses declared in the annual profit tax returns on the basis of the first-in, first-out (FIFO) method.

[587] The annual tax loss realized starting with 2024 will be recovered up to 70% of the taxable profits obtained in the next five consecutive years.

[588] Annual tax losses related to the years prior to 2024, remaining to be recovered on 31 December 2023, will be recovered up to the limit of 70% of the related taxable profits during the remaining period of recovery from the seven consecutive years to the year of recording the respective losses.

[589] Any loss incurred by a permanent establishment of a Romanian company located in an EU or Economic European Area Member State or a state that has a Double Tax Treaty in place with Romania is deductible for tax purposes from the company's revenues.

[590] Non-resident legal entities may carry forward losses attributable to their permanent establishment in Romania.

15.11 Deferred Payments, Retentions and 'Earn-Outs'

[591] Deferred payments, retentions, holdbacks and '*earn-outs*' are usually accepted and often used in Romania as a means of mitigating transaction risks.

[592] Pursuant to Romanian tax rules, the tax on capital gains derived from a transfer of assets/shares is calculated in respect of the funds effectively paid.

15.12 Acquisition Expenses

[593] In order to analyse the deductibility of a specific expense, we must first assess its correct recording in the accounts as an expense. Consequently, in those cases where the accounting rules state that the cost must be included in the value of the purchased asset, then the company will not record an expense at the moment of acquisition.

[594] Consequently, the expense will be recognized during the asset's useful life through depreciation (in the case of fixed assets) or at the moment when the asset will go out of the company's patrimony. The deductibility will be established according to the specific fiscal rules of the expense and the economic substance of the event.

15.13 Structuring the Investment: Withholding Taxes

[595] Payments to non-residents are subject to withholding taxes in Romania at the rates and on the conditions detailed below.

[596] As a preliminary note, irrespective of the various standard withholding tax rates referred to below, a 50% withholding tax will apply on income derived from Romania (e.g., interest, royalties, service fees) by non-residents in case: (i) the income is paid to countries which have not concluded an exchange of information agreement with Romania; and (ii) the transaction which generated the income is qualified as being artificial.

[597] Income earned by non-resident individuals from activities performed in Romania is generally subject to the 10% tax rate unless the more favourable provisions of a double tax treaty apply.

[598] Withholding tax (at the 16% flat rate) is levied on the following types of income sourced in Romania:

- interest, royalties and commissions received from a resident legal entity;
- interest, royalties or commissions paid by non-residents if they have permanent establishments in Romania and the interest/royalty/commission is an expense of those permanent establishments;
- income derived from sports and entertainment activities performed in Romania;
- income and fees representing remuneration received by administrators, founders or members of the Board of Directors of a Romanian company;
- income from services supplied in Romania or outside Romania of the nature of management and consultancy in any domain;
- income from services rendered in Romania, excluding international transport and related services;
- income from independent professions performed in Romania;
- prize income from contests organized in Romania;
- income obtained from liquidation of Romanian companies;
- income from the transfer of the patrimony from the fiduciary to the non-resident beneficiary.

[599] Regarding capital gains and income from real estate transactions obtained by non-resident persons, these are generally subject to the same tax treatment as residents unless the more favourable provisions of a double tax treaty apply. Depending on the details of the transaction, the intermediary (as defined by the legislation in the capital market area) or the seller may have the obligation to calculate and pay the capital gains tax from the sale of shares.

[600] With respect to special rules applicable to withholding tax on income realized by non-resident legal entities in Romania, please refer to the sections below.

15.13.1 Dividends Paid to Foreign Corporate/Group Shareholders

[601] Dividends paid to foreign corporate/group shareholders are subject to 5% withholding taxes (unless the more favourable provisions of a double tax treaty apply).

[602] Moreover, Romania has fully implemented the provisions of the EU Parent-Subsidiary Directive, pursuant to which dividends distributed by Romanian companies to companies resident in an EU Member State or in Switzerland are exempt from withholding tax if the recipient company has held a minimum of 10% of the shares of the Romanian company for an interrupted period of at least one year which ends on the date of payment of dividends. For the purpose of benefiting from the EU Parent-Subsidiary Directive, non-residents must present a tax residency certificate and an affidavit attesting compliance with the mandatory requirements provided by the EU Parent-Subsidiary Directive.

[603] Dividend and interest income obtained from Romania by EU-registered pension funds is exempt from withholding tax, provided there is a legal instrument based on which the exchange of information takes place.

15.13.2 Dividends Paid to Foreign Individual Shareholders

[604] Dividends paid to a non-resident individual shareholder are subject to 8% withholding taxes (unless the more favourable provisions of a double tax treaty apply). Please note that the provisions of the EU Parent-Subsidiary Directive are not applicable in the case of individuals.

15.13.3 Dividends Received from Foreign Subsidiaries/Affiliates?

[605] Dividends received by non-residents from foreign subsidiaries/affiliates are exempt from taxation in Romania.

15.13.4 Interest Paid to Foreign Corporate/Group Shareholders or Affiliates

[606] Interest paid to foreign corporate/group shareholders or affiliates is subject to 16% withholding taxes (unless the more favourable provisions of a double tax treaty apply).

[607] Romania has fully implemented the Interest and Royalties Directive, pursuant to which interests and/or royalties paid by a Romanian company to a company resident in another EU Member State or in Switzerland are exempt from withholding tax provided that the companies are deemed as related for a continuous period of at least two years prior to the date when the revenue is paid.

[608] An enterprise is related to another enterprise if, at least:

- the first company has a direct minimum participation of 25% in the share capital of the second company; or
- the second company has a direct minimum participation of 25% in the share capital of the first company; or
- a third company has a direct minimum participation of 25% in both companies' share capital.

[609] For the purpose of benefiting from the Interest and Royalties Directive, non-residents must present a tax residency certificate and an affidavit attesting compliance with the mandatory requirements provided by the Interest and Royalties Directive.

15.13.5 Interest Received from Foreign Corporate/Group Shareholders or Affiliates

[610] Interest payments received by non-residents from foreign corporate/group shareholders or affiliates are exempt from taxation in Romania.

15.13.6 IP Royalties Paid to Foreign Corporate/Group Shareholders or Affiliates

[611] Royalties paid to foreign corporate/group shareholders or affiliates are subject to 16% withholding tax rates (unless the more favourable provisions of a double tax treaty apply).

[612] Romania has fully implemented the Interest and Royalties Directive, pursuant to which royalties paid by a Romanian company to a company resident in another EU Member State or in Switzerland are exempt from withholding tax provided the non-resident company held, prior to the time of payment of the interest/royalty, at least 25% of the share capital of the Romanian company for a continuous period of at least two years.

[613] For the purpose of benefiting from the Interest and Royalties Directive, non-residents must present a tax residency certificate and an affidavit attesting compliance with the mandatory requirements provided by the Interest and Royalties Directive.

15.13.7 IP Royalties Received from Foreign Corporate/Group Shareholders or Affiliates

[614] Royalties received by non-residents from foreign corporate/group shareholders or affiliates are exempt from taxation in Romania.

15.13.8 Management or Consultancy Fees Paid to Foreign Corporate/Group Shareholders or Affiliates

[615] Management or consultancy fees paid to foreign corporate/group shareholders or affiliates are subject to 16% withholding taxes (unless the more favourable provisions of a double tax treaty apply). If the transaction is deemed artificial and made for tax purposes only, the tax rate will be 50%.

15.13.9 Payments to Non-residents in Respect of the Purchase or Renting of Immovable Property

[616] Payments to non-resident legal entities in respect of the purchase of immovable property are subject to the 16% CIT rate (unless the more favourable provisions of a double tax treaty apply).

[617] The seller has the obligation to declare and pay the CIT by registering for this purpose.

[618] Payments to non-resident legal entities in respect of the renting of immovable property are subject to the 16% CIT rate.

[619] In both cases, the non-resident company receiving the revenues has the obligation to register for tax purposes in Romania in order to submit the annual profit tax return.

15.14 Double Tax Treaties

[620] Romania has ratified over eighty double tax treaties concluded with various countries pursuant to which non-residents of the relevant countries may benefit from the more favourable tax rates provided by the double tax treaty concluded between Romania and the country of residence of the non-resident.

[621] In order to benefit from the more favourable provisions of the applicable double tax treaty, the non-resident must provide to the income payer, no later than the income payment date, a certificate of tax residence issued by the relevant authorities, valid for the period when the income was paid.

[622] If the conditions for applying the double tax treaty are not fulfilled, the Romanian withholding tax rates stipulated by the Romanian Fiscal Code will be applicable. A refund could be claimed, however, by the non-resident if the tax residence certificate is made available within five years following the payment of income.

15.15 Debt Financing: Deductibility of Finance Costs – Thin Capitalization

[623] Starting with 1 January 2018, the provisions regarding the deductibility of interest according to a certain level of interest rate and the amount of the degree of indebtedness of the capital were abrogated.

[624] The notion of borrowing costs is introduced, which includes:

- interest and equivalent costs;
- the payments on profit-sharing loans;

- the interests imputed on instruments (as the convertible or zero-coupon bonds);
- amounts under alternative funding mechanisms (as the Islamic finances);
- financing costs of the financing leasing payments;
- capitalized interest;
- depreciation of the capitalized interest;
- amounts calculated on the basis of a return on funding according to the transfer pricing rules;
- notional interest in derived financial instruments or of the hedging arrangements for an entity's loans;
- gains/losses from the foreign exchange differences;
- guarantee commissions for the financing mechanisms;
- brokerage commissions;
- similar costs related to fund loans.

[625] The borrowing costs resulting from transactions that do not finance the purchase/ production of fixed assets and which are carried out with affiliated persons are deducted, in a fiscal period, up to the deductible threshold of EUR500 000. This threshold does not apply to credit institutions.

[626] The total borrowing costs resulted from transactions carried out with both affiliated persons and third parties are deductible up to the threshold of EUR1 000 000.

[627] In case the threshold is exceeded, the exceeding borrowing costs (i.e., the difference between the deductible borrowing costs and the income related to the loan) are deductible in the tax period in which they are incurred up to 30% of the company's EBITDA, under specific conditions and allocations between the exceeding borrowing costs incurred with related parties and third parties.

The provisions concerning the interest limitation rule are only applicable to associated entities. Non-deductible exceeding borrowing costs can be carried forward over indefinite periods of time and deducted in future periods under the same rules.

[628] We highlight that the Romanian transfer pricing legislation mainly follows the OECD Transfer Pricing Guidelines and requires that the interest rate set between the parties has to be determined based on the market prices. In order to justify the interest rates as consistent with market prices, it should be noted that the Romanian entity has an obligation to support its transfer pricing methodology with appropriate documentation.

15.16 Transfer Pricing

[629] Transactions between related parties must be carried out at arm's length. Otherwise, the Romanian Tax Authorities have the right to adjust the taxpayer's revenues or expenses so as to reflect the market value.

[630] Transactions between Romanian and non-resident affiliated/related parties may be subject to investigation regarding compliance with transfer pricing rules.

[631] Traditional transfer pricing methods (comparable uncontrolled prices, cost plus and resale price methods, transactional net margin and profit split methods), as well as any other methods that are in line with the OECD Transfer Pricing Guidelines, may be used for setting transfer prices.

[632] Moreover, Romanian tax authorities may also consider the OECD Transfer Pricing Guidelines when applying transfer pricing rules.

[633] The local transfer pricing file must be prepared annually for large taxpayers in case the value of the transactions performed with related parties during a fiscal year exceeds one of the following thresholds (VAT excluded; exchange rate valid for the last day of the fiscal year:

- EUR350 000 for purchases/sales of tangible or intangible goods;
- EUR250 000 for services received/rendered;
- EUR200 000 for interest received/paid for financial services.

[634] As such, the term for preparing the transfer pricing file is until the deadline of submission of the annual CIT statement. Therefore, in case of a fiscal audit for *transactions exceeding the above-mentioned thresholds,* the tax authorities are entitled to ask for the mandatory transfer pricing file in ten *(calendar) days.*

[635] However, in case of transactions performed with related parties *under the mentioned thresholds or in case of small or medium-sized taxpayers*, the preparation of transfer pricing documentation is not mandatory. Notwithstanding, the tax authorities may request it, but the deadline for (preparing and) presenting it will be from thirty to sixty (calendar) days, plus an extension of the deadline (if requested by the taxpayer) with a maximum of thirty days (i.e., overall, maximum ninety days).

[636] Failure to meet the obligation to make the transfer pricing file available to the fiscal authorities can be subject to fines ranging between RON12 000 and RON14 000 for big and medium-sized taxpayers and fines ranging between RON2 000 and RON3 500 for other taxpayers.

[637] Moreover, in the event that taxpayers are not able to support their transfer pricing methodology with appropriate documentation, Romanian tax authorities have the right to adjust the taxpayers' revenues and expenses at market value. This aspect will trigger CIT adjustments (and, if the case, VAT), as well as the related interests and penalties. For the purpose of having more certainty with respect to the pricing policy to be implemented between related parties, taxpayers carrying out transactions with related parties can request the issuance of an Advance Pricing Agreement (APA) from the Romanian tax authorities.

[638] The APA is issued for a period of up to five years (in exceptional cases, it may be issued for a longer period for long-term agreements) and is binding on the tax authorities, provided no substantial changes occur with respect to the critical assumptions.

[639] If taxpayers do not agree with the content of the APA, they can notify the Romanian tax authorities with respect to their disagreement within thirty days, in which case, the agreement does not produce legal effects.

16 EMPLOYMENT CONSIDERATIONS

16.1 Legislative Framework

[640] Labour relations in Romania are governed mainly by Law no. 53/2003 on the Labour Code, republished in the Official Gazette no. 345 of 18 May 2011, as further amended and supplemented (the '*Romanian Labour Code*'), which contains mandatory provisions regarding labour relations and establishes minimum employee rights.

[641] The framework affecting labour and employment in Romania also includes various other pieces of legislation, such as:

- Law no. 367/2022 on social dialogue, published in the Official Gazette no. 1238 of 22 December 2022 (the '*Romanian Social Dialogue Law*').
- Law no. 67/2006 regarding the protection of employee rights on the transfer of an undertaking, or units or parts thereof, published in the Official Gazette no. 276 of 28 March 2006 (the '*Law 67/2006*'), which transposes into Romanian legislation the Council Directive 2001/23/EC of 12 March 2001 on the approximation of the laws of the Member States relating to the safeguarding of employees' rights in the event of transfers of undertakings, businesses or parts of undertakings or businesses, published in the Official Journal of European Communities no. L 082 of 22 March 2001 (the '*Acquired Rights Directive*').
- Law no. 467/2006 setting out the general framework on informing and consulting employees, published in the Official Gazette no. 1006 of 18 December 2006 (the '*Law 467/2006*').
- Government Decision no. 905/2017 on the general employee register, published in the Official Gazette no. 1005 dated 19 December 2017, as further amended and supplemented (the '*GD 905/2017*').

[642] In addition, collective bargaining agreements may be concluded at the sector of activity level, at the group of companies' group level or at a company level. Collective bargaining agreements are legal documents of mandatory and general application.

16.2 Employment Protection

16.2.1 Continuity on Business Transfers

[643] Law 67/2006 defines the transfer as 'a transfer of ownership from the transferor to the transferee over an undertaking, business, or part thereof, *having the* *objective of pursuing the central or ancillary economic activity*, whether or not they are operating for gain' (our emphasis).

[644] The factual assessment for the qualification of a transfer of an undertaking, business or part thereof falls under the jurisdiction of the national court, and when interpreting the national law, the judge should consider the criteria for interpretation set out by the case law of the EU Court.

[645] In the light of the EU Court case law, for a transfer within the meaning of the Acquired Rights Directive to exist, two conditions must be met:

- there must be a change of employer – i.e., there must be a change, in terms of contractual relations, in the legal or natural person who is responsible for carrying on the business and who incurs the obligations of an employer towards employees of the entity; and
- maintenance of the identity – the maintenance of the identity is marked both by the continuation by the new employer of the same or similar activities and by the continuity of its workforce, its management staff, the way in which its work is organized, its operating methods or the operational resources available to it.

16.2.2 Automatic Transfer

[646] Under Law 67/2006, the rights and obligations of the transferor, as employer, arising from the individual employment agreements concluded with the transferred employees and from the applicable collective bargaining agreement in existence at the date of transfer, are transferred in full to the transferee. Such transfer takes place automatically on the date of the transfer of the undertaking, business or part thereof, and it may not be postponed to another date.

[647] The case law of the EU Court has confirmed the principle of automatic transfer, taking the view that the transfer procedure under the Acquired Rights Directive is a matter of public policy from which neither the transferor nor the transferee can be exempt.

16.2.3 Employee Representation

[648] Romanian law does not provide any right for the employees to have representatives on the management bodies of the employer.

[649] Nevertheless, employers may invite the representative trade union at company level to participate in the board of directors or other assimilated bodies in order to discuss problems of professional, economic and social interest. The decisions of the board of directors or of other assimilated bodies regarding the problems of professional, economic and social interest must be communicated in writing to the trade union within two days from the date of the meeting.

[650] Also, for the purpose of defending the rights and promoting the professional, economic and social interests of its members, representative trade unions should receive from employers the information necessary for the negotiation of collective bargaining agreements.

16.3 Information and Consultation

16.3.1 Transfer of Shares

[651] In principle, a transfer of shares does not in itself trigger any information or consultation obligation.

[652] However, under Law 467/2006, any company with at least twenty employees must inform and consult the trade union/employees' representatives on various aspects regarding the situation of the company, as follows:

- the recent and probable development of the company's activities and economic situation;
- the situation, structure and probable development of employment within the company and any anticipated measures, in particular where there is a threat to employment; and
- decisions which may lead to substantial changes in the organization of the work, contractual relationships or labour relations, including those provided under Romanian law regarding specific information and consultation procedures in cases of collective dismissal and of the transfer of a business.

[653] The information and consultation procedure under Law 467/2006 does not entitle the employees to block a transaction.

[654] Law 467/2006 does not provide for any specific deadlines but only for certain principles related to the timeframe of the information and consultation procedure.

[655] Thus, the information must be made at a time in a manner and having a content allowing the trade union/employees' representatives adequately to examine the issue and to prepare for the consultation.

[656] The consultation must take place:

- at a time, in a manner and having content allowing the trade union/employees' representatives to adequately examine the issue and to prepare a point of view;
- at a relevant level of representation of the management and of the trade union/employees' representatives, taking into consideration the subject matter of the consultation;
- based on the information provided by the employer and of the point of view that the trade union/employees' representatives are entitled to prepare;
- in a manner allowing the employees to meet the employer and to obtain a purposeful answer to any point of view they may submit; and

- with a view to negotiating an agreement in respect of the decisions that may lead to important changes in the organization of the work, contractual relations or labour relations.

[657] The means of information and consultation of employees may be freely determined at any time, by collective bargaining agreements and understandings entered into in accordance with the law.

[658] Employers are not obliged to disclose information or initiate consultations if such are of a nature which might severely damage the operation of the company or its interests. The decision not to disclose such information or not to initiate consultations must be discussed in front of the employees' representatives. If the employees' representatives consider such decision without proper foundation, they may refer this issue to the competent courts of law.

[659] Additional information and consultation aspects may be regulated under collective bargaining agreements, if applicable.

16.3.2 Sale of Business

Informing the Transferee

[660] Prior to the transfer, the transferor has an obligation to notify the transferee of all the rights and obligations to be transferred to the latter. However, failure to comply with such obligation does not affect the transfer of such rights or obligations or the rights of any employees.

Information and Consultation of the Employees

[661] The transferor and the transferee are under the obligation to inform in writing their respective trade unions/employees' representatives or, if no such trade unions/employees' representatives are in place, their respective employees directly, at least thirty days prior to the date of the transfer, on the following aspects:

- the date or proposed date of the transfer;
- the reason for the transfer;
- the legal, economic and social implications of the transfer for the employees;
- the measures envisaged in relation to the employees; and
- the working and employment conditions.

[662] In addition, where the transferor or the transferee envisages measures in relation to its employees, it should consult the trade unions/employees' representative with a view to reaching an agreement at least thirty days prior to the date of the transfer.

[663] Romanian legal writers consider that such obligation of consultation with a view to reaching an agreement is limited to the obligation to negotiate in good faith and not an obligation to effectively reach such an agreement.

16.3.3 Trade Unions

[664] The Romanian legal system guarantees the right of employees to form trade unions and gives the trade unions substantial powers and key roles with regard to labour-related matters.

[665] Trade unions are set up for the purpose of defending the rights of their members, deriving, *inter alia*, from the labour legislation, collective bargaining agreements and individual employment agreements before courts, jurisdictional bodies, and other state institutions and authorities.

[666] Trade unions have the right to use specific means, such as negotiation, procedures for settlement of disputes by mediation, arbitration or conciliation, petitions, protests, meetings, demonstrations and strikes, under the conditions provided for by the law.

[667] Trade unions negotiate and conclude collective bargaining agreements.

[668] Trade unions have the right to undertake any action provided by law, including bringing an action to court on behalf of their members, based on special and written powers of attorney from such members. The action may not be brought or continued by the trade unions if the person concerned explicitly opposes or renounces the trial.

16.3.4 Employees' Representatives

[669] In those cases where employers have more than ten employees but where no representative trade unions are established, the employees' interests may be promoted and defended by their representatives elected and authorized expressly for such purpose.

[670] The main attributions of the employees' representatives are the following:

- to pursue compliance with the employees' rights in accordance with applicable legislation, applicable collective bargaining agreements, individual employment agreements and internal regulation;
- to participate in the drawing-up of the internal regulation;
- to promote the employees' interests regarding salaries, working conditions, duration of work and leave days, stability at work, as well as any other professional, economic and social interests related to labour relations;
- to notify the labour authorities regarding any breach of legal provisions and of the collective bargaining agreements; and
- to negotiate a collective bargaining agreement.

16.3.5 General Obligation Regarding the Information and Consultation of Employees

[671] Employees are entitled to be informed and consulted in relation to any corporate transactions in the cases provided under Law 467/2006, as detailed above.

16.3.6 Information and Consultation Procedure in Cases of Collective Dismissal

[672] The Romanian Labour Code provides for the special protection of employees affected by collective dismissal by requiring a joint effort of the employer, the relevant employee representative bodies and the labour authorities aimed at finding solutions to avoid the dismissals, to reallocate the employees in question with the same or other employers or, finally, to award severance payments as provided by the law and applicable collective bargaining agreements. The collective dismissal rules apply:

(a) for employers which have more than 20 but less than 100 employees, if a minimum of 10 employees are affected during a thirty-day period;
(b) for employers which have at least 100 but less than 300 employees, if a minimum of 10% of the employees are affected during the thirty-day period; and
(c) for employers which have at least 300 employees, if a minimum of 30 employees are affected during a thirty-day period.

Information and Consultation of the Trade Union/Employees' Representatives

[673] If the employer intends to proceed with collective dismissals, it must initiate, in due time and for the purpose of reaching an agreement, a consultation with the trade union/the employee's representatives in respect of at least the following issues:

- ways and means to avoid the collective dismissal or to reduce the number of employees to be dismissed; and
- reduction of the consequences of the collective dismissal by social measures related, among others, to professional re-qualification or re-training of the dismissed employees.

[674] During the consultations, the employer must provide all relevant information and must notify the trade union/the employees' representatives in writing, for the purpose of allowing them to prepare their proposals in due time, as to various issues related to the collective dismissal, as such matters are provided for under the Romanian Labour Code (e.g., the reasons for the envisaged dismissal, the total number and categories of employees involved, the number of employees affected by the collective dismissal, the criteria for establishing the priority order for dismissal, the measures for alleviating the consequences thereof, the compensation to be paid).

[675] A copy of the notification referred to above must be submitted by the employer to the territorial labour inspectorate and to the territorial agency for the employment of labour force on the same date as the notification of the trade union/ the employees' representatives.

[676] The trade union/the employees' representatives may propose to the employer measures for avoiding collective dismissal or for decreasing the number of dismissed employees within ten calendar days from receipt of the notification. The employer must answer in writing and justify such proposals within five calendar days from the date of their receipt.

Notification of the Labour Authorities

[677] In cases where, after consulting the trade unions/the employees' representatives, the employer decides to apply the collective dismissal measures, the employer must notify the territorial labour inspectorate and the territorial agency for the employment of labour force in writing in this respect.

[678] Such notification must include all relevant information relating to the intention to proceed to collective dismissal, as provided under the Romanian Labour Code, as well as the results of the consultations with the trade union/the employees' representatives, in particular the reasons for the collective dismissal, the total number of employees involved, the number of the employees affected by the collective dismissal and the date from which or the period during which the dismissals are to take place.

[679] The employer must communicate a copy of the said notification to the trade union/the employees' representatives on the same date as the date of its communication to the territorial labour inspectorate and the territorial agency for the employment of labour force.

[680] The trade union/the employees' representatives may transmit any opinions to the territorial labour inspectorate.

[681] The dismissal decisions may only be issued at least thirty days following the notification of the labour authorities as referred to above.

[682] Upon the justified request of one of the parties, the territorial labour inspectorate, after consulting the territorial agency for the employment of labour force, may: (a) reduce the term for the issue of the dismissal decisions; or (b) extend such term (by ten calendar days at most, if the issues related to the collective dismissal may still not be settled as at the date initially established).

[683] During this period, the territorial agency for the employment of labour force must seek solutions to the issues related to the collective dismissal and communicate these solutions in due time to the employer and to the trade union/the employees' representatives.

[684] The Romanian Labour Code establishes the minimum protection that must be ensured for the employees and does not allow derogations to the detriment of the employees.

[685] In this respect, the Romanian Labour Code stipulates that employees may not waive the rights recognized by the law. Any transaction aiming at the waiver or limitation of the rights recognized by the law to the employees is sanctioned with nullity.

16.3.7 Methods of Termination of Employment

[686] Under Romanian law, employment agreements may be terminated in one of the following ways:

- *ipso jure* – in certain situations set forth by the Romanian Labour Code, such as absolute nullity of the employment agreement or the expiry of an employment agreement concluded for a definite period of time;
- by the parties' mutual agreement; and
- at the initiative of one of the parties (i.e., either at the employee's initiative, by way of resignation, or by the employer's initiative, by way of dismissal).

16.3.8 Termination of Employment at the Employer's Initiative

[687] Employers may dismiss an employee only in limited cases and following the procedures set out by the law, either for reasons related to the employee's person or for reasons not related to the employee's person.

Dismissal for Reasons Related to the Employee's Person

[688] Employers may dismiss an employee for one of the following reasons related to such employee:

- the employee's gross negligence or the employee's repeated breach of the work discipline rules or of those set out in the individual employment agreement, the applicable collective bargaining agreement or the internal regulation, as a disciplinary sanction (further to a preliminary investigation procedure);
- temporary detention of the employee or detention at his/her domicile for a period of time exceeding thirty days on the conditions provided by the criminal procedure code;
- the employee's physical and/or mental disability to perform his/her work, as ascertained by a decision of the competent bodies (having the relevant medical expertise); and
- professional unsuitability (further to a preliminary appraisal of the employee).

Dismissal for Reasons Not Related to the Employee

[689] Dismissal for reasons not related to the employee is represented by the termination of the employment due to the elimination of the job position occupied by the employee for one or more reasons not related to the employee's person (e.g., economic reasons or reorganization of the employer). The elimination of the job position must be effective and have a genuine and serious cause.

16.3.9 Rights Against Dismissal and/or Compensation on Termination

Interdictions to Dismiss

[690] Under the Romanian Labour Code, dismissal of employees is prohibited:

- based on criteria related to sex, sexual orientation, genetic characteristics, age, nation, race, colour, ethnic group, religion, political beliefs, social origin,

handicap, family situation or responsibilities, trade union membership or activity; and
- for exercising, in accordance with the law, the right to strike or other trade union rights.

[691] Also, the dismissal of employees is prohibited in the following cases:

- during a period of temporary incapacity to work, as certified by a medical certificate in accordance with the law;
- during quarantine leave;
- during the pregnancy of the employee, insofar as the employer had knowledge of it prior to issuing the dismissal decision;
- during a maternity leave;
- during a childcare leave for children up to two years old or, in the case of a disabled child, up to three years;
- during a childcare leave for children up to seven years old or, in the case of a disabled child, for inter-current disease, up to eighteen years;
- during the employee's annual leave; and
- during paternity leave and career leave or during absence from work for unforeseen circumstances (caused by a family emergency due to illness or accident, which makes the employee's immediate presence indispensable, subject to prior notification of the employer and with recovery of the period of absence until the employee's normal working hours have been fully covered).

Notice Period in Case of Dismissal

[692] The statutory or contractual notice period applies. The minimum notice period provided under the Romanian Labour Code is twenty business days.

Severance Payments and Other Protection Measures

[693] The Employees who are dismissed for reasons not related to their person will benefit from active measures against unemployment and may benefit from compensation under the conditions provided by the law and by applicable collective bargaining agreements.

Offer of a Vacant Position Within the Employer

[694] Under the Romanian Labour Code, in certain cases of termination of employment (i.e., in case of termination of the employment agreement for professional unsuitability or for physical or psychical inaptitude, as well as further to the admission of a reinstatement request of a person who was unlawfully dismissed), the employer has the obligation to propose to the employee other workplaces which are vacant and compatible with the professional background of the employee or, as the case may be, with the ability to work established by the labour medical physician. If the employer does not have any vacancies available, it must request the support of the territorial employment agency with a view to the redeployment of the relevant employee.

Risks Related to the Cancellation of the Dismissal Decision

[695] An employee may challenge a dismissal decision within forty-five calendar days from the date he/she receives such decision (regarding measures ordered relating to the conclusion, execution, modification, suspension or termination of the individual employment agreement, including commitments to pay sums of money), respectively within thirty calendar days from the date he/she receives such decision (on disciplinary sanctions related cases).

[696] A successful appeal triggers the invalidation of the dismissal decision with the payment by the employer of damages equal to all increased and updated salaries and additional benefits to which the employee may have been entitled as of the dismissal date. In addition, upon the employee's request, the court deciding the invalidation of the dismissal may order the reinstatement of the employee at his/her previous workplace with the employer.

Restrictions Related to New Employments Following Collective Dismissals

[697] Under the Romanian Labour Code, during a period of forty-five days from the time of the dismissal, the employees dismissed by collective dismissal have the right to be reemployed with priority at their workplaces to take up any positions eradicated but then reinstated by the employer, without any test, contest or trial period.

[698] In accordance with the general principle referred to above, no derogation from the minimum rights of the employees set out in the Romanian Labour Code is allowed.

[699] The termination of employment is governed by the same legal rules irrespective of whether the dismissed employees are 'blue-collar workers' or 'white-collar workers'.

[700] However, additional rights may be negotiated by the employees under their individual employment agreements.

16.4 Procedures to Be Followed on Termination

[701] The Romanian Labour Code provides for specific procedures to be followed in case of dismissal, depending on the reason for the dismissal, such as the preliminary investigation procedure (in cases of disciplinary dismissal), preliminary appraisal of the employee (in cases of dismissal for professional unsuitability) and information and consultation procedures (in cases of collective dismissal).

[702] Also, the Romanian Labour Code provides for certain provisions that must be included in the dismissal decision under sanction of nullity.

16.4.1 Minimum Salary at National Level

[703] The mandatory minimum gross base salary in Romania is currently RON3 300 (approx. EUR665) per month for full-time employees.

[704] The mandatory minimum gross base salary is regularly updated based on government decisions.

16.4.2 Mandatory Social Contributions

[705] The main social security contributions owed by the employer and the employee under Romanian law are those set out in the table below:

Type of Insurance	*Employer (1)*	*Employee (2)*	*Total (1+2)*
	Social Contributions		
Social security insurance (CAS)	N/A for normal working conditions 4% for difficult working conditions 8% for special working conditions (e.g., mine units, civil aviation)	25%	25% for normal working conditions 29% for difficult working conditions 33% for special working conditions (e.g., mine units, civil aviation)
Health insurance (CASS)	N/A	10%	10%
Contribution for labour insurance	2.25%	N/A	2.25%
Income tax	N/A	10%	10%

16.4.3 Collective Bargaining Agreements

[706] Under Romanian law, trade unions and employers' associations may negotiate and enter into collective bargaining agreements. Employers hiring at least twenty-one employees are required to negotiate a collective bargaining agreement at company level (but not to complete such negotiations and enter into a collective bargaining agreement).

[707] Collective bargaining agreements may not include provisions less beneficial to the employees than those established by agreements concluded at a higher level.

[708] Any individual employment agreement entered into in Romania must observe the minimum employee protection requirements set out in the applicable collective bargaining agreements.

[709] As a general rule, in cases where the law, the individual employment contract, the collective bargaining agreements or the internal regulations stipulate different rights, the most favourable right for the employee should be applied.

16.4.4 Power of Trade Unions

[710] Trade unions are typically strong in formerly state-owned companies, and this usually results in a broad range of additional benefits for the employees, further to collective negotiations.

16.5 Pensions

[711] The public social security system is governed by Law no. 263/2010 on the unitary public pension system ('*Law 263/2010*').[5]

16.5.1 Affiliation

[712] Romanian and/or foreign citizens and/or stateless persons having their domicile or residence in Romania may be insured under the Romanian public pensions system.

[713] Law 263/2010 regulates relevant categories of persons who are insured in the public pensions system by the effect of the law and therefore have the obligation to pay social contributions and the right to receive social insurance benefits under Law 263/2010, such as:

- persons employed under individual employment agreements;
- public officers;
- other persons obtaining incomes assimilated to salaries for which social insurance contributions are due, in accordance with the Fiscal Code;
- persons carrying out elective functions or who are appointed with executive, legislative or judicial authority throughout the duration of their mandate;
- unemployed persons who receive monthly incomes paid from the unemployment insurance fund; and
- persons obtaining incomes from independent activities and/or copyright, for which social contributions are due.

[714] Persons who do not fall under the scope of Law 263/2010 may nevertheless choose to affiliate voluntarily with the public pension system.

16.5.2 Contributions Payment

[715] The social security contributions are established by law depending on the work conditions and are distributed between the employee and the employer, as detailed above (please refer to the section related to mandatory social contributions).

[5] Law 263/2010 in force from 1 Jan. until 31 Dec. 2023 partially replaced by Law 223/2015 and repealed and replaced by Law 127/2019.

[716] Employers must calculate and pay on a monthly basis to the social insurance budget the employer's contributions, on the one hand, and the individual employees' contributions, on the other hand.

16.5.3 Contribution Stage

[717] The minimum contribution period is, as a rule, fifteen years for both men and women (to be reached by January 2030 for women and reached in March 2015 for men, further to a gradual increase set out under Law 263/2010).

[718] The complete contribution stage is, as a rule, thirty-five years for both men and women (to be reached by January 2030 for women and reached in March 2015 for men, further to a gradual increase set out under Law 263/2010).

16.5.4 Standard Retirement Age

[719] The standard retirement age is, as a rule, 65 years for men and 63 years for women (to be reached by January 2030 for women and already reached in March 2015 for men, further to a gradual increase set out under Law 263/2010).

16.5.5 Retention of Key Management and Employees

[720] As regards employees, under the Romanian Labour Code, employees may not be prevented from resigning from an employer, subject to a notice period which may be set (based on the individual employment agreement) at a maximum of forty-five business days for management positions and at a maximum of twenty business days for non-management positions.

[721] Non-compete clauses may be included in individual employment agreements (as detailed below), in which case the possibility of a former employee performing certain activities for a competitor may be restricted for a limited period of time.

[722] As regards directors, members of the board of directors and managers (to whom the management of the company has been delegated by the board of directors) of Romanian joint-stock companies appointed pursuant to the Company Law, such key persons may not be employees of the company. Instead, mandate or management agreements should be concluded with the persons holding such positions (which agreements are not subject to the restrictive provisions of the Romanian Labour Code).

16.5.6 Non-compete Clauses in Individual Employment Agreements

[723] Under the Romanian Labour Code, upon the execution or during the performance of an individual employment agreement, the parties may negotiate and include in the agreement a non-compete clause prohibiting the employee from performing, after the termination of the individual employment agreement, in his/her own interest or in the interest of a third party, an activity competing with those

performed for the former employer, in consideration of a monthly pecuniary compensation paid by the employer for the duration of the non-compete clause.

[724] The non-compete clause will be effective provided that the individual employment agreement specifically provides for:

- the activities prohibited to the employee;
- the amount of the pecuniary monthly compensation (the negotiated monthly pecuniary compensation must be at least 50% of the average gross salary revenues received during the six months prior to the termination of the individual employment agreement or, if the duration of the individual employment agreement was less than six months, of the average monthly gross salary revenues received throughout the duration of the individual employment agreement);
- the duration of the non-compete obligation (it being specified that the non-compete clause may take effect for a maximum two-year term from the termination of the individual employment agreement);
- the third parties for whose benefit the activities may not be performed;
- the geographical area where the non-compete clause will be applicable (and where the employee may be in real competition with the employer).

[725] The non-compete clause may not have the effect of completely preventing the exercise of the employee's profession or specialization.

[726] The competent court may diminish the effects of the non-compete clause upon demand of the employee or of the labour authorities.

[727] The non-compete clause is not applicable in those cases where the individual employment agreement is terminated at the employer's initiative for reasons not related to the employee or in certain cases where the employment agreement is terminated *ipso jure* (such as dissolution of the employer or absolute nullity of the employment agreement).

16.6 Treatment of Foreign Employees

[728] EU, EEA and Swiss nationals have the right to work in Romania without any work permit being necessary for such purpose.

[729] Under Romanian law, a foreigner other than EU, European EEA and Swiss nationals may enter into an individual employment agreement only if he/she holds a work permit and a stay permit for working purposes issued by the Romanian General Inspectorate for Immigration.

[730] Work permits are not required for persons who will *not* perform their activity in Romania based on individual employment agreements but based on management/mandate agreements, such as directors, members of the board of directors and managers (to whom the management of the company has been delegated by the board of directors) of Romanian joint-stock companies or directors of limited liability companies, appointed pursuant to the Romanian Company Law no. 31/1990. However, such persons will have to obtain long-term stay visas and long-term stay permits.

16.6.1 Work Permits and Stay Permits: Requirements Applicable to Foreigners Other than EU, EEA and Swiss Nationals

[731] For the purpose of this section related to work permits and residency permits, 'foreigner' or 'foreign citizen' means a person other than EU, EEA and Swiss nationals.

[732] Foreigners who intend to work in Romania as employees or as secondees must follow the main procedural steps outlined below:

(1) Obtaining a work/secondment permit from the Romanian General Inspectorate for Immigration.

Work permits/secondment permits are issued/delivered for the following categories of workers: (a) permanent workers; (b) seconded/detached workers; (c) inter-company transferee (ICT) (d) seasonal workers; (e) trainee; (f) cross-border workers; and (g) highly qualified workers.

The work permit for permanent workers gives the holder the right to conclude a full-time individual employment agreement for a fixed term or for an indefinite term with a single Romanian employer (natural person or legal entity) or representative office, branch or subsidiary in Romania of a foreign legal entity.

The secondment permit gives the holder the right to work, for a period up to one year in a minimum five-year period, under the terms of the secondment decision, from a foreign employer to a Romanian employer or to a representative office, a branch or a subsidiary in Romania of a foreign legal entity.

The ICT permit gives the holder the right to work, for a period of up to three years, under the terms of the secondment decision, from a foreign employer to a Romanian employer, part of the same group of companies as the foreign employer.

(2) Obtaining a long-term stay visa from the diplomatic missions and consular offices of Romania.

Long-term stay visas are granted for a ninety-day period for certain purposes provided by the law, including employment, secondment or 'other purposes'.

Long-term stay visas grant foreigners the temporary right to stay in the territory of Romania and the possibility to request the extension thereof by obtaining a stay permit.

(3) Obtaining a stay permit from the Romanian General Inspectorate for Immigration.

After having obtained the work permit/secondment permit and the long-term stay visa, but in any case, prior to the expiry of the long-term stay visa, foreigners also need to obtain a stay permit.

In practice, the formalities related to such procedures may take from three to six months and do not involve significant fees (e.g., a fee of EUR100 in RON equivalent must be paid for the issue of the work permit for a permanent worker, a fee of EUR25 in RON equivalent must be paid for the issue of the work permit for a seasonal worker).

16.7 Taxation of Foreign Employees

[733] Foreign employees, tax residents or non-residents in Romania, locally employed by a Romanian employer and working in Romania, are taxable in Romania with effect from their first day of activity in Romania. In this case, the payroll will be conducted by the Romanian employer, and full social security contributions and income tax will be due (10% income tax, 35% – employees' social security contributions and 2.25% – employer's social security contributions).

[734] Separately from the above, according to Romanian legal provisions, an individual without domicile in Romania becomes taxable in Romania on his/her worldwide income starting the date any of the Romanian residence criteria below are met:

- centre of vital interests (closest personal and/or economic ties) in Romania; and
- physical presence in Romania for a period or periods which exceed in aggregate 183 days in any twelve-month period ending in the calendar year concerned.

[735] In addition, as per Order 1099/2016 of the Romanian Ministry of Public Finances, concerning the individual's Romanian tax residency, an expatriate present in Romania for more than 183 days has the obligation to file a standard questionnaire within thirty days after meeting the residency criteria (e.g., within thirty days after he exceeded the 183 days of presence in Romania). The standard questionnaire should be accompanied by supporting documents, referable to the specific status of the individual, on a case-by-case basis.

[736] Based on the questionnaire and the supporting documents, the competent Romanian tax authorities will issue, within thirty days, a decision regarding the tax residency status in Romania of the individual.

[737] If the decision indicates that the individual qualifies as a tax resident in Romania, then he/she will be liable to declare and pay taxes on his/her worldwide income in Romania.

16.8 Liability of Directors

[738] Generally, the Company Law stipulates that directors/members of the board of directors are jointly liable to their company for: (i) the existence of the payments for share capital contributions; (ii) the existence of the paid dividends; (iii) the existence of the registers required by law and their correct holding; (iv) the accurate fulfilment of the resolutions of general meetings; and (v) strict fulfilment of the duties which the law and the constitutive act imposes.

[739] Moreover, directors/members of the board of directors are liable to their company for damages caused by agreements signed/executed by managers or personnel when the damage would not have occurred had they fulfilled their supervisory duties as imposed by their position. Nonetheless, directors are jointly liable with their immediate predecessors if, being aware of irregularities committed by the latter, they do not communicate such irregularities to the auditors or, where appropriate, to the internal auditors and financial auditors.

[740] As regards joint-stock companies, the Company Law obliges each director/member of the board of directors to conclude a professional liability insurance. This obligation also applies to members of the managing board and supervisory board. Directors/members of the board of directors of limited liability companies do not have an obligation to conclude a professional liability insurance policy but may choose to do so.

[741] An extensive range of criminal offences is laid down by the Company Law applicable to directors/members of the board of directors – a responsibility that cannot be covered through an insurance policy.

17 ACCOUNTING TREATMENT

[742] Most Romanian entities apply Romanian Accounting Standards in compliance with European Accounting directives drawn up by the Ministry of Finance (regulations approved by Order of the Ministry of Public Finance no. 1802/2014).

[743] For credit institutions, non-banking financial institutions, payment institutions and electronic money institutions, insurance companies and private pension companies, accounting standards are drawn up by specific authorities, with the assessment of the Ministry of Finance.

17.1 IFRS

[744] Credit institutions (including Romanian branches of foreign credit institutions), companies listed on a regulated market and non-financial institutions are obliged to apply the International Financial Reporting Standards (IFRS).

17.2 Accounting Treatment for Business Combinations

[745] The norms enacted through Ministry of Public Finance Order no. 897/2015 provide for the application of a specific accounting treatment for mergers, spin-offs, dissolutions and liquidations of companies and for the withdrawal or exclusion of shareholders from companies.

[746] Entities involved in a merger or other business restructuring (split-off, liquidation, dissolutions, withdrawal or exclusion of shareholders) are required to apply specific accounting treatment for such transactions.

[747] For company acquisitions (the purchase of one business or company by another company by taking over the assets or the ownership equity of the acquired entity), no specific accounting treatment is required.

[748] The application of the specific accounting treatment provided for a merger, spin-off, dissolution and liquidation of companies and to the withdrawal or exclusion of shareholders from companies is limited only to those companies involved in such transactions.

[749] Consequently, entities other than those companies referred to above are not eligible to apply the above-mentioned specific accounting treatment.

[750] Where there is a share-for-share acquisition, no merger relief applies pursuant to Romanian accounting standards.

[751] In cases of merger by absorption, companies involved in the merger are evaluated in order to determine the share exchange ratio at a specific time, pursuant to different methods, such as those based on the accounting values (net assets methods) or those based on fair values (method based on results, cash-flow method, stock method, etc.).

[752] Assets and liabilities transferred from the acquired company to the acquiring company further to the merger must be booked by the acquiring company at the value resulting from evaluation.

[753] In cases of business transfer, the overall business is evaluated in order to determine the selling price. However, the acquiring company is required to evaluate each acquired asset and liability in order to determine the fair value. The difference between the selling price and the net asset (assets – liabilities) has to be recognized as goodwill.

[754] For both scenarios (merger and business transfer), changes in assets or liabilities resulting from the intention of the acquirer or from events after the acquisition do not affect the value at which the acquired assets and liabilities are booked by the acquirer at the acquisition date.

17.3 Provisioning

[755] Provisions are liabilities of uncertain timing or amount. An entity must recognize a provision if but only if:

- a present obligation has arisen as a result of a past event;
- payment is probable (‘*more likely than not*’); and
- the amount can be estimated reliably.

17.4 Goodwill

[756] Goodwill is generally recognized as a balance sheet item and represents the difference between the purchase price and the fair value, applicable on the transaction date, of the net assets purchased by an entity.

[757] If the goodwill is treated as an asset, the goodwill is amortized generally over a maximum of a five-year period. However, entities may amortize the goodwill systematically over a period exceeding five years, provided that this period does not exceed ten years and that this period is presented and justified in explanatory notes.

[758] The life of acquired goodwill (or goodwill arising on consolidation) cannot be regarded as 'indefinite' (and therefore not subject to amortization).

17.5 Recognition of Intangible Assets

[759] Pursuant to Romanian Accounting Standards, an intangible asset is an identifiable non-monetary asset without material support.

[760] In order to meet the criteria to be identified, the asset must be separable or must arise from contractual/other legal rights.

[761] For intangible assets held in or on a physical object (i.e., compact disc, legal documentation, tape), in order to classify them as fixed/intangible assets, the entity must evaluate which component is more significant.

[762] An intangible asset must be recognized on the balance sheet if it is estimated that it will generate economic benefits for the entity and its cost can be assessed in a credible manner.

[763] A specific case is represented by assets resulting from an internal project. In order to recognize an asset, the company must evaluate the capacity of the asset to generate economic benefits.

[764] Pursuant to Romanian Accounting Standards, the following elements qualify as intangible assets: incorporation expenses; development expenses; concessions, patents, licences, trademarks, similar rights and assets (except for those created internally by the entity); goodwill; advance payments made to suppliers of intangible assets; intangible assets for the exploration and valuation of mineral resources and other intangible assets.

17.6 Depreciation of Intangible Assets

[765] Intangible assets are depreciated over different periods of time, depending on the specific useful life of the intangible asset, as follows:

(a) incorporation expenses recognized as intangible assets must be depreciated over a maximum of five years;
(b) development expenses recognized as intangible assets must be amortized over the contract duration or over the usage period, as the case may be (c) concessions recognized as intangible assets[6] are depreciated over the duration of the usage of the concession, established pursuant to the agreement; and
(c) patents, licences, trademarks, rights and other similar assets are depreciated over the duration stipulated for their usage by the entity holding such assets.

17.7 Negative Goodwill

[766] Negative goodwill is generally recognized as a balance sheet item and represents the difference between the transaction costs and the fair value, at the transaction date, of the net assets purchased by an entity.

[767] However, provided that the negative goodwill is reported to expected future losses and expenses, which are identified in the acquisition plan of the purchaser and these may be credibly measured but do not represent identifiable debts on the acquisition date, that part of the negative goodwill must be recognized as income in the profit and loss account when these losses and future expenses are recognized.

[768] Provided that the negative goodwill is not reported to expected future losses and expenses, which may be credibly measured on the acquisition date, this negative goodwill must be recognized as income in the profit and loss account, as follows:

(1) the value of the negative goodwill that does not exceed the fair values of the acquired non-monetary, identifiable assets must be recognized as income when the future economic benefits included in the identifiable amortizable assets acquired are consummated, hence, over the remaining useful life of these assets; and
(2) the value of the negative goodwill exceeding the fair values of the non-monetary, identifiable assets must be recognized immediately as income.

17.8 Treatment of Acquisition Costs

[769] As a general rule, acquisition costs related to a business transfer or a merger must be expensed in the period in which they are incurred. However, the accounting provisions entitle a company to capitalize the set-up costs subject to two conditions:

---

[6] If the agreement stipulates the payment of a royalty/rent fee, instead of an amortizable value, then the accounting records of the entity benefiting of the concessions will reflect the expense representing the royalty/rent fee, without recognizing an intangible asset.

(1) such set-up cost must be written off within a maximum five-year period; and
(2) no distribution of profits is allowed before the set-up costs are completely written off, except if the amount of distributable reserves and/or retained earnings is at least equal to the unamortized set-up costs.

17.9 The Effective Date of Acquisition

[770] In the case of mergers, the effective date of acquisition is set by the Company Law, which stipulates that the merger takes effect:

(1) when one or several new companies are incorporated, on the date of incorporation of the new company or of the latest company to be incorporated;
(2) in other cases, on the date of registration of the resolution of the last general meeting of shareholders that approved the operation, except in cases where the agreement between the parties stipulates that the transaction will take place at another date (which may not be subsequent to the end of the ongoing financial period of the acquiring company or beneficiary companies and which may not be prior to the closure of the last closed financial period of the company/ies that transfer/s its/their patrimony).

[771] For a business transfer, the effective date of acquisition is the date stipulated in the sale contract.

17.10 Valuation of Deferred and/or Contingent Consideration Payments

[772] Contingent payment obligations are generally considered when the acquired company/business is evaluated.

[773] From an accounting perspective, contingent payment obligations assumed by the acquirer must be booked off-balance sheet and reviewed on an ongoing basis.

17.11 Recognition of Profit on Sale

[774] In the case of business transfers, the profit related to the sale must be recognized on the date when the sale is carried out, pursuant to the date stipulated in the sale and purchase contract.

[775] In the case of a merger by absorption, a profit or a loss appears in the absorbed company only when methods based on fair values are used for the valuation of the companies involved in the merger. Such profit or loss represents the difference between the fair value of the net asset and the accounting value of the net asset and must be recognized in the P&L account when the merger becomes effective pursuant to law.

18 FUTURE DEVELOPMENTS

[776] According to *Investing in CEE, Inbound M&A report* 2022/2023 published by Mazars, the top four countries for M&A deal volume in the CEE in 2022 were Poland (with 235 deals), Austria (120), the Czech Republic (81) and Romania (76). Deal volume in Romania outperformed expectations in 2022 with 76 transactions, up 17% from 65 in 2021. Aggregate value, however, almost halved from EUR2.7 bn to EUR1.4 bn.

[777] The political outlook seems rather stable after a more bumpy start, and there are no foreseeable laws negatively affecting M&A.

www.ingramcontent.com/pod-product-compliance
Lightning Source LLC
Chambersburg PA
CBHW071349230926
51846CB00002B/490
9789403530383